The Digital Revolution Transforming Tomorrow's World

Oliver Kensington

Copyright © [2023]

Title: The Digital Revolution Transforming Tomorrow's World

Author's: Oliver Kensington

All rights reserved. No part of this publication may be reproduced, stored in a retrieval system, or transmitted in any form or by any means, electronic, mechanical, photocopying, recording, or otherwise, without the prior written permission of the publisher or author, except in the case of brief quotations embodied in critical reviews and certain other non-commercial uses permitted by copyright law.

This book was printed and published by

ISBN:

For permission to reproduce any of the material in this book

Table of content

Chapter name **Page No**

1. The Digital Revolution — 1
2. The Role of Technology in Organisational Change — 37
3. The Effects of New Technologies on Society — 56
4. Learning and Technology in the Classroom — 69
5. The Rise of the Digital Health Sector — 84
6. Modern Media and Entertainment — 99
7. Urban Planning and Smart Cities — 117
8. Technology and the Future of Work — 134
9. Cyber Risks and Online Dangers — 152
10. Sustainability in the Environment and Cutting-Edge Technology — 170

Chapter 1:
The Digital Revolution

1.1- Introduction to the digital revolution

This is Chapter 1, "Digital Innovation in Its Historical Context."

Thinking back on the historical events and technological landmarks that led to the information era is the first step on the road to the digital revolution. This chapter takes us on a wonderful journey through time, from the creation of the first computer to the advent of the internet.

The Birth of Computing: The history of the first computers and the people who created them.

The Information Age: How the transition from analogue to digital representation of information altered our ability to share and preserve information and to tackle difficult challenges.

The Internet Era: the beginning of the World Wide Web and the advent of worldwide connection that has fundamentally altered society.

How smartphones changed our lives The Mobile Revolution.

The Digital Ecosystem, Part 2

We explore the intricate system that constitutes the digital revolution in this chapter. Everything that makes up the digital world is examined, from its hardware to its software, its networks to its data centres.

Computer hardware has come a long way from bulky mainframes to portable cellphones.

Software Revolution: The impact of software on the digital landscape and the breadth of its possible uses.

An in-depth exploration of the servers and interconnected networks that make the World Wide Web possible.

With the advent of the digital age and the development of big data analytics, data has become a highly prized commodity.

Transforming Industries — Chapter 3

The advent of digital innovation has had far-reaching consequences for many sectors, causing the collapse of some business models while spawning entirely new ones. The chapter focuses on the ways in which the digital revolution has affected many industries.

The growth of e-commerce and its impact on the retail sector are discussed.

Financial technology (fintech) and the banking industry's digital transformation.

Telemedicine and the Future of Healthcare: How New Technologies Are Changing the Face of Medical Care.

Entertainment and Media: The evolution of streaming services and the transition from analogue to digital media.

Fourth Chapter: The Effects of Digital Innovation on Society

The advent of digital technology has altered not only business practises but also the very fabric of society. In this chapter, we examine how technological progress has affected society in the areas of communication, relationships, and activism.

The impact of social media on our social lives and how we interact with one another.

Digital Activism: The impact of technology on grassroots movements for social and political change.

Ethical Considerations: Investigating the moral quandaries brought up by the Internet, such as data privacy, fake news, and online conduct.

Education and Online Study (5th Chapter)

The educational sector has also felt the effects of the digital revolution. In this chapter, we take a look at how innovative tools like virtual classrooms and online education platforms are changing the face of academia.

A look back at how education has changed over time and how technological advancements have impacted the field.

E-learning Platforms: Examining the benefits and drawbacks of online education platforms.

How AI is influencing the future of education through personalised instruction and data-driven insights.

The Impact of Technology on Healthcare Delivery (Chapter 6)

The introduction of cutting-edge digital technologies has revolutionised healthcare. Telemedicine, wearable tech, and data-driven healthcare solutions are all discussed in this chapter.

Telemedicine and remote healthcare: how digital technology is expanding access to medical care, particularly in underserved areas.

Wearable Technology: The impact of wearables on health tracking and management.

The application of AI to healthcare tasks such as diagnosis, treatment planning, and medication discovery.

Chapter 7: Media and Entertainment for the Internet Age

The digital age has brought about revolutionary changes in the entertainment and media industries. The impact of digital media, social media, video games, and virtual reality on our leisure time is discussed in this chapter.

The emergence of online video streaming services and their effect on broadcast and theatrical releases.

How the rise of social media has become a major force in influencing mainstream culture.

The development of the gaming business and the exciting possibilities of virtual reality for gamers.

Urban Planning and Smart Cities, Part 8

The effects of digital innovation are not confined to specific sectors; they are also changing the face of our cities. This chapter delves at the idea of smart cities and the ways in which the proliferation of digital technologies is enhancing city life.

'Smart City Infrastructure," which includes the Internet of Things, aims to make cities more sustainable, efficient, and connected.

Sustainable urban development: the role of technological advancement in eco-friendly city planning.

The importance of data analytics in enhancing municipal services and administration Data-Driven Decision-Making.

Chapter 9: The Digital Workforce of Tomorrow

The digital revolution is having a dramatic effect on the workplace. In this chapter, we'll take a look at how things like telecommuting, robotics, and technology have altered the workforce.

Remote employment and the Gig Economy: Opportunities and constraints in today's increasingly popular employment arrangements.

Automation and Artificial Intelligence: The effects on occupations and sectors.

Strategies for individuals and businesses to advance their skills and compete in the modern labour market.

Digital security and threats are the topic of Chapter 10.

The prevalence of cyberattacks has grown in tandem with the digital universe. In this chapter, we'll look at why cybersecurity is crucial, what kinds of threats exist, and how to defend against them.

Cybersecurity is becoming increasingly important in today's interconnected world.

Malware, phishing, and ransomware are just some examples of the different types of cyber risks that exist.

Strategies and best practises for protecting data and systems, both individually and organizationally.

Chapter Eleven: "Digital Innovation and Environmental Sustainability"

The information technology revolution can help solve some of the world's most pressing environmental problems. In this chapter, we look at the role that digital solutions and environmentally friendly technologies are playing in ensuring the planet's survival.

Green Technology: advancements in alternative energy sources, energy-saving gadgets, and environmentally responsible methods.

The role of digital solutions in lowering carbon emissions and fighting global warming.

The importance of technology firms in encouraging socially and ecologically sound business practises.

The first eleven chapters of the book are summarised below; each chapter deals with a different facet of the digital revolution and its far-reaching implications.

1.2- Historical context and technological milestones

First, we'll take a look at the digital ecosystem.

Now that we live in the digital age, every aspect of our existence is intertwined with the huge and complex digital environment. The interconnected technology, physical infrastructure, and service providers that make up this ecosystem are what make our digital lives possible. In this section, we'll examine the various components of this ecosystem and the role they play in shaping our contemporary environment.

New Hardware Developments -- Part 1

Hardware, or the physical equipment and components used in the processing and storage of digital information, is the backbone of the digital ecosystem. The expansion of the information age is largely attributable to advances in hardware.

Starting with the gigantic mainframes of the middle of the 20th century and ending with today's pocket-sized smartphones, we will discuss the evolution of computer hardware.

Moore's Law, which states that the density of transistors on integrated circuits would double approximately every two years, has fueled fast improvements in computer power.

The broad acceptance of digital technology may be traced back to the rise of personal computing, which began with the advent of the first personal computers in the 1980s.

Mobile Devices: The development of mobile devices, from the first cell phones to today's smartphones, has had a significant impact on our daily lives.

Revolution in Software, Part 2

Digital technology relies on hardware to function, but software is the unseen power behind it. There would be no functional digital environment without software in some way.

The Birth of Programming: We investigate the early programming languages and the pioneers who created the first lines of code as we delve into the history of software development.

The evolution of operating systems like UNIX, Windows, and Linux has influenced the way we use computers and other electronic gadgets.

The Graphical User Interface (GUI): GUIs transformed how we engage with computers, opening the doors to a wider audience.

The growth of application software has made it possible to perform a wide variety of digital jobs, from word processing to video editing.

Part 3: The Backbone of the Internet

The internet is the lifeblood of the digital ecosystem because it links together individuals, machines, and information from all over the world. To fully comprehend today's digital ecosystem, one must have a firm grasp on the underlying architecture that makes the internet possible.

Beginning with ARPANET and progressing to the creation of the TCP/IP protocol suite, we delve into the history of networking.

Tim Berners-Lee's development of the World Wide Web in 1989 radically altered people's ability to find and share information online.

The internet wouldn't be able to function without the vast data centres where all of the information we create every day resides and is managed.

Cloud Computing: The advent of cloud computing has revolutionised how organisations and people handle data and service storage and delivery.

Part Four: Information Is the New Oil

The digital ecology would collapse without data. Decisions, innovations, and the services we rely on every day would not be possible without it. The importance of data in the modern digital age will be discussed here.

Data Creation and Collection: We investigate the numerous data sources, from sensors and social media to online transactions, that feed the ever-expanding digital data universe.

Data analytics and insights have entered a new era thanks to the concept of big data, which is defined by its volume, velocity, and diversity.

Concerns regarding privacy and security in the data environment have arisen in tandem with the explosion of available information. The necessity of protecting private data is discussed.

The discipline of data analytics has expanded rapidly in recent years, providing businesses with invaluable insights into consumer habits, market tendencies, and operational efficiencies.

Section 2: The Evolution of Business

The effects of the digital revolution extend far beyond the realm of technology itself, reshaping entire markets and presenting previously unimaginable opportunities. In this chapter, we'll look at how the digital revolution has affected many industries.

Part 1: Stores and Online Markets

With the rise of online shopping, the retail sector has undergone a dramatic change. The rise of e-commerce has revolutionised not only the way we shop, but also the very nature of stores themselves.

We explore the history of e-commerce, from the first online marketplaces to the current domination of sites like Amazon in our feature length documentary, The Rise of E-commerce.

Altering Consumer Behaviour: The advent of online buying has raised customers' expectations for ease, rapidity, and customization.

Omnichannel Retail: the merging of traditional brick-and-mortar stores with online marketplaces.

Adapting to the digital world presents many obstacles for traditional shops, but e-commerce also presents many opportunities.

Part 2: Money and Financial Technology

With the rise of fintech firms and the digitization of financial services, the financial industry has been hit by a wave of digital disruption.

Fintech's Roots: We examine where fintech came from and how it has expanded to include anything from online payment systems to robo-advisors.

Digital Banking: The proliferation of online financial institutions and mobile banking apps has fundamentally altered the way in which we handle our money.

Blockchain technology and cryptocurrencies like Bitcoin have the potential to radically alter the financial services industry.

Concerns concerning regulatory oversight and consumer protection have been brought to light by the digitalization of the financial sector, which presents regulatory challenges.

Part 3: Medical Care and Remote Monitoring

Digital innovation is also having a profound effect on the healthcare industry. The way we get and give medical attention is evolving as a result of developments in telemedicine, wearable technologies, and data-driven healthcare solutions.

The Telemedicine Revolution: Telemedicine has gained popularity, particularly in underserved and rural areas.

Fitness trackers and smartwatches are just two examples of the wearable technology that is helping people keep tabs on their health and make positive changes as a result.

Artificial intelligence is being applied in healthcare for things like diagnosis, medicinal research, and individualised care.

Privacy and Security in Healthcare: Protecting patients' personal information is of the utmost importance, and we explore the difficulties inherent in doing so.

Chapter Four: "Media and Entertainment in the Internet Age"

Streaming services, social networking, video games, and virtual reality have all contributed to a sea change in the entertainment and media industries.

The proliferation of streaming services has changed the business model for distributing media like films and TV shows.

Influencer Culture and the Rise of Social Media: Online communities have rapidly evolved into major nodes for the production, distribution, and promotion of material.

Virtual and augmented reality have helped the gaming business reach a wider audience and create more engaging games.

Examining the difficulties of IP protection in the digital age and the effects of piracy on the media business, we present Intellectual Property and Piracy.

Third Chapter: The Effects of Digital Innovation on Society

The impact of the digital revolution is not limited to the business sector; it has also altered the nature of society. In this section, we explore the ramifications of digital innovation on society, namely its effects on interpersonal interactions, group dynamics, and political mobilisation.

First, we'll talk about the online social scene.

The ways in which we make connections, share information, and express ourselves are all profoundly influenced by the prevalence of social media in our daily lives.

In this section, titled "The Social Media Landscape," we look at the key social media platforms, their development, and the impact they have had on worldwide communication.

The significance of one's digital identity to their privacy and their online standing.

Filter Bubbles and Echo Chambers: How algorithms affect what we see and the dangers of closed communities.

The effects of social media on psychological well-being, including addiction and cyberbullying.

Second Part: Online Protests

As a result of the internet, people are more politically active than ever before. Online communities have evolved into potent spaces for activism, awareness-building, and policy change advocacy.

The effects of significant online advocacy campaigns are discussed, including #BlackLivesMatter and #MeToo.

The Arab Spring: How social media played a part in the uprisings and what it means for the future of political mobilisation.

Digital Censorship and Surveillance: The Obstacles Facing Activists in the Face of Governmental Surveillance of Digital Spaces.

Understanding how viral information may inspire action and spark societal change.

The Ethical Considerations section follows.

Privacy, fake news, and online conduct are just a few of the ethical issues that have surfaced in the digital age. Here, we take a look at some of the moral challenges posed by the information age.

Privacy loss due to increased monitoring and data collection in the Internet age.

The influence of the digital dissemination of incorrect information on public debate.

Cyberbullying and other forms of online harassment have real-world repercussions that should not be ignored.

The responsibility of tech giants to address ethical issues and encourage responsible technology use is the subject of The Ethical Responsibilities of Tech Companies.

Part IV: Teaching and Learning in the Digital Age

The digital revolution has not spared the world of education. This chapter looks at how innovative tools like online classrooms and virtual learning environments are changing the face of education.

Chapter 1: How Schooling Has Changed Over Time

The impact of digital innovation in education can only be understood in the context of the field's long and eventful history.

Traditional Education: A look at the advantages and disadvantages of more conventional schooling methods.

Distance Learning: How the advent of modern technology has broadened the scope of this time-honored idea of education.

The Growth of Online Education Platforms: How these have contributed to making education more widely available around the world.

Blended learning is the practise of combining online and face-to-face instruction in today's classrooms.

Part 2: Online Courseware

The proliferation of e-learning platforms means that students of all ages and from all walks of life have access to a wealth of educational materials.

We look at the forerunners of online education, such Khan Academy and Coursera, in The Pioneers of Online Learning.

Massive Open Online Courses (MOOCs): How Free and Open Online Courses (FOCs) Are Changing the Face of Higher Education Around the World.

Technology-enabled, individualised learning for each student is the focus of the term Personalised Learning.

The problems and criticisms of online education, such as worries about quality and accessibility.

Part Three: Artificial Intelligence's Impact

From tailor-made curriculums to computer-generated grades, AI is quickly becoming an indispensable tool in the classroom.

The role of artificial intelligence in tailoring instruction to each individual learner, including how AI algorithms can sift through student records in search of useful insights.

Virtual Classrooms: The utilisation of virtual classrooms powered by artificial intelligence to promote distance education and teamwork.

EdTech Startups: The proliferation of new businesses using technology to improve education by incorporating elements of artificial intelligence.

Ethical Considerations: issues regarding bias and data privacy associated with the use of AI in the classroom.

Section 4: Predicting the Future of Online Education

The field of digital learning will develop in tandem with the progress of technology. Here, we take a stab in the dark at predicting what might happen next.

Virtual reality's potential to transform classroom instruction into a fully immersive experience is explored in this insightful article.

What blockchain technology could mean for the future of verifying and sharing credentials in higher education.

Lifelong Learning: What it means to pursue education throughout one's entire life, and what role digital platforms will play in this process.

The power of online education can level the playing field for students all around the world and make a quality education available to all.

Chapter 5: The Rise of the Digital Health Industry

Through technological advancement, the healthcare industry has undergone a revolutionary change. In this chapter, we look at how data-driven healthcare solutions like telemedicine, wearable tech, and mHealth apps are altering traditional approaches to patient care.

Part 1: The Rise of Telemedicine

When it comes to providing healthcare to people in rural or underserved areas, telemedicine has quickly become a standard practise.

We explore the origins of telemedicine and its early implementation in The Emergence of Telemedicine.

How telemedicine's "remote consultations" put patients in touch with doctors without leaving home.

Extending the reach of telemedicine to other areas of healthcare, such as mental health and chronic disease management.

Legal and Regulatory Considerations: The difficulties of, and rules pertaining to, telemedicine, such as licencing and payment.

Part 2: Mobile Health Apps

Fitness trackers and smartwatches are just two examples of the wearable tech that is enabling people to take responsibility of their own health and wellness.

In The Rise of Wearables, we delve into the development and rising acceptance of wearable medical gadgets.

How wearables monitor a user's health by recording data on their heart rate, steps taken, and quality of sleep.

Medical-grade Wearables: The research and development of wearable medical devices for use in diagnosis and monitoring of health.

Privacy and Data Security: The significance of protecting personal health information gathered through wearables.

Part 3: The Role of AI in Medical Care

AI is making great strides in the medical field, opening up exciting new avenues for diagnosis, treatment planning, and medication development.

Medical imaging data analysis using AI algorithms for disease identification in its early stages.

The use of AI to personalise medicine based on a patient's unique characteristics and genetic information.

Drug Discovery and Development: The use of AI to hasten the process of finding new and better medicines.

The ethical concerns and regulatory barriers associated with the application of AI to healthcare.

Section 4: Protecting Individual Information When Using Digital Healthcare

Patients' privacy and the safety of their medical records are becoming increasingly important issues as healthcare increasingly moves online.

The Health Insurance Portability and Accountability Act (HIPAA) and its function in safeguarding patient data: a brief introduction.

Cybersecurity in healthcare: how susceptible healthcare networks are to hacking and data leaks.

Debate persists over who should have access to and ownership of patients' personal health information (Patient Consent and Data Ownership).

The potential for blockchain technology to safeguard and centralise electronic health records The Future of Digital Health Records.

Chapter 6: Media and Entertainment for the Internet Age

The digital age has brought about revolutionary changes in the entertainment and media industries. The impact of digital media, social media, video games, and virtual reality on our leisure time is discussed in this chapter.

Part 1 Streaming Services

The ascent

The introduction of streaming services has altered the landscape of television and film distribution, giving viewers an array of previously unavailable options.

We track the rise of streaming services and their effect on traditional television networks in The Streaming Revolution.

How streaming firms have put resources into creating original programming to win over viewers.

 Cord Cutting: The movement towards dropping traditional pay-TV in favour of online video.

Streaming services have been rapidly expanding, penetrating new areas throughout the world (The Global Reach of Streaming).

Part 2: Online Communities and the Influencer Economy

The growth of the "influencer culture" may be traced back to the proliferation of social media as a central place for content production, user interaction, and commercial promotion.

The Social Media Landscape: We examine the most popular social media sites, who uses them, and how they shape people's habits on the web.

What we mean by "Content Creators and Influencers" is the phenomenon of ordinary people and famous people building up sizable fan bases and making money off of them.

The Advertising Ecosystem: How Sponsored Content and Influencer Marketing Are Changing the Face of Business Today.

Fandom and Online Communities: the phenomenon of people coming together online because of a common interest in a fandom.

Part 3: Virtual Reality and Video Games

With the advent of cutting-edge technologies like virtual and augmented reality, gaming has gone from being a specialised pastime to a widely popular entertainment option.

From arcades to home consoles and mobile gaming, we cover it all in The Evolution of Gaming.

Esports and Competitive Gaming: The development of esports into a mainstream spectator sport.

What is Virtual Reality (VR) and how is it being utilised to make games and other experiences more lifelike?

Augmented Reality (AR): The ability of AR to bridge the gap between the virtual and the real.

Chapter Four: Intellectual Property and Counterfeits

Copyright, piracy, and fair use are all topics that have arisen as a result of the need to safeguard intellectual property in the digital age.

In this age of digital replication and distribution, it might be difficult to uphold copyright rules.

The prevalence of digital piracy and its effects on content providers and businesses.

What impact do streaming services and licencing deals have on the income of content creators?

Fair Use and Remix Culture: The Grey Area of Transformative Works and Copyright Violations.

Section 7: Urban Planning and Smart Cities

The effects of digital innovation extend beyond specific sectors to the built environment as a whole. This chapter delves at the idea of smart cities and the ways in which the proliferation of digital technologies is enhancing city life.

Infrastructure for the Internet of Things and Smart Cities

The Internet of Things (IoT) is crucial to smart city initiatives because it facilitates the interconnection of many systems and devices to improve the liveability, sustainability, and connectivity of urban areas.

We explore the entire ecosystem of the Internet of Things, from sensors to connection to data analytics.

Smart Transportation: The ways in which the Internet of Things (IoT) is being used to upgrade transportation networks, lessen traffic jams, and boost public transportation.

Energy Efficiency: The application of Internet of Things (IoT) devices to control, measure, and improve the effectiveness of energy use in structures.

Environmental Monitoring: the use of IoT to monitor atmospheric conditions and other environmental factors in populated regions.

Part 2: Urban Sustainability

The advent of the digital age has heralded a new era of sustainable urban planning that places a premium on green policies and measures.

Green Building Technologies — Breakthroughs in eco-friendly architecture, energy-saving materials, and eco-friendly building methods.

Renewable electricity Integration: the incorporation of solar and wind power into municipal electricity networks.

What advantages digital technology is bringing to garbage management and recycling.

Sustainable Transportation entails efforts to expand access to environmentally friendly modes of transportation including electric vehicles and bike-sharing networks.

Section 3: Making Choices Based on Available Information

Data analytics and real-time information are becoming increasingly important for modern cities to make educated decisions and enhance their services.

The creation of "Smart City Dashboards" that offer municipal officials with real-time monitoring data on a variety of urban metrics.

Predictive Analytics: How this cutting-edge field is assisting urban centres in foreseeing and resolving pressing concerns like traffic congestion and citizen security.

Information is used to improve anything from garbage collection to emergency services.

Protecting individuals' personal information and privacy during the rollout of smart city technologies is of paramount importance.

Eighth Chapter: Work in a Digital World's Future

Remote work, automation, and shifting employment patterns in the digital age are fundamentally altering the nature of labour. The effects of these changes are discussed in this chapter.

Part One: Freelancing and the "Gig" Economy

The rise of the gig economy and general acceptance of remote work have given employees more options for how they can earn a living.

The Rise of Remote Work: How Technological Progress Has Facilitated Working From Home.

The pros and cons of remote work, from the perspective of both people and companies.

The effects of the gig economy on conventional forms of work are examined in The Gig Economy.

The practise of working remotely while travelling the world, often known as "digital nomadism."

Part 2: Artificial Intelligence and Robotics at Work

Automation and AI are reshaping the workplace in ways that could boost productivity but also upend established hierarchies and occupations.

What we call The Automation Revolution is the automation of mundane and repetitive tasks in all sectors of the economy.

How artificial intelligence is being used in decision-making, data analysis, and forecasting market trends.

The effects of automation on the labour force and the consequent need for retraining and professional development are discussed in Job Disruption and Reskilling.

The ethical issues that arise with implementing AI in the workplace, such as discrimination and job loss.

Skills Development for the Information Age Labour Market

Individuals and businesses alike must flex with the changing labour market or risk falling behind. Methods to maintain one's value in today's digital labour market are discussed here.

The concept of lifelong learning and its importance in the modern information age.

Upskilling and retraining have never been easier than with the proliferation of online learning and professional development opportunities.

Corporate Training Programmes: How Businesses Invest in the Future of Their Workers.

The Future of Workspaces : The importance of both traditional and digital work environments in adapting to the future of work.

Part Four: Balance and Health at Work

employment-life balance and the health of employees have grown increasingly important as employment has moved online and away from physical locations.

How the Internet and other digital tools can improve and even erase the traditional barriers between work and leisure time.

The effects of working remotely on mental health and methods for preventing deterioration are discussed in Mental Health and Remote Work.

Unplugging from technology (a.k.a. "digital detox") is a strategy for relieving mental and emotional strain and finding greater fulfilment in life.

The Future of Well-being at Work: Innovative Approaches to Promoting Well-being in the Digital Workplace.

Cybersecurity and Digital Threats Chapter 9

The importance of cyber security is growing in tandem with the digital universe. In this chapter, we will discuss the expanding relevance of cybersecurity, the many forms of cyber threats, and methods for mitigating them.

The Increasing Relevance of Cybersecurity (Section 1)

The importance of safeguarding digital assets is growing as we increasingly rely on them in our daily lives.

An overview of the ever-changing cybersecurity threat landscape The Digital Threat Landscape.

The Price of Cyberattacks: The monetary and reputational losses that victims and businesses experience as a result of cybercrime.

The importance of government, industry, and cybersecurity professionals working together is emphasised.

Cybersecurity expertise are in high demand to ensure the safety of our digital infrastructure.

Cybersecurity Threats, Part 2

The best way to protect yourself from cyberattacks is to familiarise yourself with the many types of cyberthreats. In this article, we'll take a look at the most frequent cyber threats and the holes they exploit.

Infection techniques used by malware like as viruses, worms, and ransomware are explored in Malware.

Phishing: The practise of social engineering and other methods used by cybercriminals to entice victims into divulging personal information.

Data Breaches: the means by which hackers bypass security measures and get unauthorised access to private data.

Denial-of-service (DoS) attacks, or the interference with services by flooding systems with traffic, and methods to prevent them.

Section 3: Digital Asset Protection

This section offers advice on how to keep your data, systems, and networks secure in the digital world.

The importance of firewalls and antivirus software in warding off cyberattacks.

Multi-factor authentication (MFA): Why it's crucial to use it to protect your online accounts.

Importance of educating workers on cybersecurity best practises through training and awareness programmes.

The creation of incident response plans to deal with cyber incidents efficiently is referred to as Incident Response Plans.

Part Four The Government's Part and International Cooperation

Governments and international organisations have a vital role in establishing standards and implementing cybersecurity measures because of the widespread nature of the problem.

Overview of national cybersecurity plans and the government's role in ensuring the safety of vital networks and systems.

The significance of international agreements and collaboration in the fight against cyber threats.

The importance of having rules and compliance systems in place to maintain acceptable levels of cybersecurity.

Cybersecurity in the future: what we can expect in terms of new dangers and technologies.

Sustainability of the environment and technological advancement make up Chapter 10.

The benefits of technological advancement extend beyond the realm of human convenience and efficiency to include mitigating harmful effects on the natural world. In this chapter, we look at the role that digital solutions and environmentally friendly technologies are playing in ensuring the planet's survival.

Part 1: Eco-Friendly Innovations

Environmentally friendly and long-lasting technological advancements are collectively known as "green technology."

Innovations in solar, wind, and hydroelectric power generating constitute the field of study known as "renewable energy technologies."

The creation of more efficient appliances and lights is referred to as Energy-efficient Appliances.

Sustainable materials, designs, and methods of constructing are all part of what are known as "Green Building Practises."

Environmental Monitoring : the practise of using electronic sensors and computational methods to keep tabs on the natural world around us.

Subsection 2: Cutting Carbon Output

The world has made reducing carbon emissions a top priority, and digital technology is helping immensely.

Electric Vehicles (EVs): The proliferation of EVs and their potential to lessen global warming pollution.

Creating "smart grids" that streamline both production and consumption of power.

Carbon capture and storage (CCS) refers to methods used to collect and safely store carbon dioxide.

Climate Modelling: the practise of making use of computer models and simulations to investigate the causes and consequences of climate change.

Sustainability and Technology Organisations (Section 3)

The world's largest technology corporations are increasingly investing in programmes and policies that aim to reduce their impact on the environment.

Carbon Neutrality Pledges: Commitments by major technology companies to become carbon neutral and lessen their impact on the environment.

How tech businesses are investing in renewable energy procurement to fuel data centre operations.

Sustainable Supply Chains: Efforts made to establish such a network, cut down on waste, and recycle electrical and electronic equipment.

Green Innovations: the creation of environmentally friendly items including energy-saving gadgets and recyclable packaging.

Chapter Four: "The Circular Economy"

The goal of the circular economy is to maximise the recycling and reusing of resources while simultaneously decreasing waste.

The difficulty of dealing with e-waste and recycling electronic equipment.
 Product Lifecycle Analysis: Methods for Evaluating a Product's Total Impact on the Environment.
 Sustainable Materials: The research and development of environmentally friendly electrical and packaging materials.

What consumers can do to encourage companies to adopt more sustainable practises is discussed under the heading "Consumer Awareness and Responsibility."

This excerpt covers the first ten chapters of the book, omitting the introduction and the chapter on technological and historical landmarks, and delves into numerous facets of the digital revolution and its revolutionary effects on our world.

1.3- The impact of the digital age on society and industries

The Effects of Technology on Business and Culture

Introduction

The extensive acceptance and integration of digital technologies into various parts of society and industry defines the digital age, also known as the Information Age or the Information Revolution. The ways in which we interact, work, study, and live have all been profoundly impacted by this shift. Computers, the internet, and mobile devices have created a new era of global connectedness and information availability. In this in-depth investigation, we'll examine the many ways in which the digital age has changed our culture and economy, from the good to the bad.

The Digital Revolution: Introduction

1.1 The Inception of Electronic Computers
The first digital computers were created in the middle of the twentieth century, marking the beginning of the digital age. The theoretical groundwork for digital computing was built by pioneers like Alan Turing and John von Neumann, and the creation of powerful computers was made possible by the advent of the transistor and integrated circuits in the 1950s and 1960s.

1.2 The Explosion of Online Activity
In the late 20th century, the internet, which had its beginnings as a military research project, exploded in popularity around the world. Tim Berners-Lee's invention of the World Wide Web in 1989 ushered in a new era of instantaneous global communication and changed the way information was shared forever.

The Rise of Mobile Technology 1.3
The emergence of mobile devices like smartphones and tablets in the 21st century was a watershed moment for the Internet Age. These gadgets are now commonplace, allowing people to stay in constant contact and gain access to information no matter where they may be.

Effects on Interpersonal Interactions

2.1 How Digital Technology Is Changing Speech and Language
The advent of the digital age has revolutionised human communication by making it more convenient, widespread, and

expressive. It's hard to imagine our daily lives without email, social media, and instant messaging.

The Impact of Social Media, Version 2.2

The ways in which we communicate with one another, disseminate information, and express ourselves have been profoundly altered by the advent of social networking sites like Facebook, Twitter, Instagram, and LinkedIn. The social and political effects of these mediums have been far-reaching.

2.3 Difficulties and Prospects in Interpersonal Communication

While there are many upsides to digital communication, there are also downsides such as cyberbullying, fake news, and invasions of privacy. These challenges must be met as society takes advantage of digital communication's benefits.

Third Chapter: Repercussions for Business and Labour

3.1 The Impact of Technology on the Workplace

Globally, businesses have adopted digital technologies to improve efficiency, cut costs, and standardise procedures. The advent of AI and data analytics has changed the face of labour dramatically.

3.2 Freelancing and the "Gig" Economy

The gig economy emerged as a result of the rise of digital technologies that made it possible for people to work remotely on short-term projects. The traditional employment model, including job stability and benefits, may be affected by this change.

Online Shopping and Electronic Commerce 3.3

The proliferation of online shopping has caused shifts in customer habits and retail business models, causing havoc for conventional stores. E-commerce pioneers like Amazon have changed the face of the retail industry.

Implications for Teaching and Learning

4.1.1 E-Learning and Online Courses
The widespread availability of online courses and resources is one way in which the digital age has transformed the educational system. While e-learning platforms have expanded educational opportunities to more people, they have also prompted concerns about the effectiveness of online education.

4.2 Computer Literacy and Data Saturation
Digital literacy is increasingly important as the amount of data available online grows. It is up to individuals to deal with information overload, identify reliable from unreliable sources, and form an informed opinion.

4.3 Trends in Education's Near Future
Virtual reality, augmented reality, and adaptive learning technologies are just a few examples of how the digital era is changing the face of education. The way we educate future generations may be drastically altered by these innovations.

The Repercussions for Healthcare Systems

5.1 Remote Healthcare and Telemedicine
Telemedicine is made possible by the development of digital technology, which now permits patients to get medical advice and treatment at a distance. The current outbreak of COVID-19 has made this a pressing concern.

5.2 Confidentiality of Health Records
Large volumes of health data have been generated in the digital age, which raises serious concerns regarding patient privacy, data security, and the appropriate application of healthcare data.

5.3.1 New Medical Developments

Breakthroughs in fields like genomics, drug development, and personalised medicine have been made possible by the advent of digital technologies, which have sped up medical research and innovation.

Effects on the Entertainment Industry and the Media

Digital Content and Streaming Services 6.1
Streaming services like Netflix, Hulu, and Disney+ have revolutionised the entertainment business in the digital age. The television and movie industries have been shaken up by these platforms.

6.2 User-Generated Content and Social Media
The emergence of user-generated content on platforms like YouTube and TikTok has given individuals the power to produce and share their own media, threatening established media gatekeepers.

6.3 Intellectual Property and Copyright
Copyright and intellectual property protection face new obstacles in the digital age due to concerns over piracy and fair use.

Effects on Confidentiality and Safety

Surveillance and Data Privacy Issues
Concerns regarding data privacy have arisen in the digital era due to the increased collection and sharing of personal information by businesses and governments. Major problems have arisen from the rise of surveillance and data breaches.

7.4 Cybersecurity and Potential Dangers
Cybersecurity is now a major issue because of how dependent we are on digital technologies. Individuals, businesses, and governments alike are vulnerable to cyberattacks, ransomware, and other forms of malicious software.

Questions of Morality

Surveillance, data ownership, and the moral use of technology are only few of the digital age's ethical hot button topics. These moral quandaries are ones that society must address.

Effects on Representative Government and Democracy

8.1 Political and Social Movements in the Digital Age

Political participation has been revolutionised by the advent of the digital era, which has facilitated the rapid expansion of social movements and political involvement via internet channels. Black Lives Matter and the Arab Spring are two such movements.

8.2 Fake News and Disinformation

The rise of disinformation and fake news on social media platforms has damaged trust in institutions and impacted elections, posing challenges to democracy.

8.3 Government Surveillance and Civil Liberties

The government's monitoring programmes have prompted worries about civil liberties and privacy rights despite being justified on the grounds of national security.

Future of Technology in the Information Age

9.1 Up-and-Coming Technologies

Emerging technologies like blockchain, quantum computing, and 5G are shaping the future of the digital era. These innovations may cause widespread changes in many fields.

9.2 Moral and Legal Structures

There is a rising need for ethical principles and regulatory frameworks to deal with the difficulties and dangers posed by technology as the digital era develops.

9.3 Equity and Digital Inclusion

Access to digital technology is becoming increasingly crucial for education, employment, and civic involvement, hence efforts must be done to assure digital inclusion and equity.

Tenth Chapter: A Wrap-Up

To sum up, the advent of the digital age has remodelled many aspects of human life, including how we interact socially, professionally, educationally, and recreationally. While it has improved communication and productivity, it has also raised concerns about personal information safety and ethical considerations. Building a digital future that is more inclusive, equitable, and sustainable requires finding a middle ground between taking use of digital technology's benefits and avoiding its drawbacks as we continue to traverse this disruptive era.

Chapter 2:
The Role of Technology in Organisational Change

2.1- How businesses are adapting to the digital age

The Digital Transformation of Business

Businesses' operations, interactions with customers, and ability to compete on a global scale have all been profoundly affected by the arrival of the digital age. In this era of rapid technological development, businesses that don't keep up with the times run the risk of being left in the dust. Businesses of all sizes and in all industries need to adopt digital strategies and technology if they want to succeed in the modern economy. Focusing on major trends, challenges, and opportunities that have evolved in this fast shifting landscape, this talk will investigate how organisations are adjusting to the advent of the digital age.

1. The Necessity of Digital Transformation

For good cause, "digital transformation" has become a popular catchphrase in the corporate world. It's the broad strategy wherein companies use digital technologies to radically alter their internal processes, interactions with customers, and business models. The shift to digital is now essential and cannot be avoided.

Digital technologies are being adopted by businesses in many different areas.

a. Operational Efficiency: Simplifying in-house operations via automation and data-driven decision making. For instance, manufacturing organisations are adopting IoT (Internet of Things) sensors to monitor equipment health and optimize production.

b. Customer-Centricity: Enhancing customer experiences through tailored marketing, e-commerce, and AI-driven chatbots. Retailers, for example, apply data analytics to understand consumer behavior and preferences better.

c. Innovation and Product Development: Employing electronic means to quicken the pace of innovation and the introduction of new items to the market. Tech businesses like Apple consistently develop their product offerings, delivering new products and software updates often.

d. Supply Chain Optimisation: utilising digital platforms to monitor the flow of merchandise, enhance logistics, and guarantee accurate stock levels at all times. Supply chain management has been revolutionised by sophisticated algorithms used by companies like Amazon.

Online marketplaces and electronic trade

The proliferation of online shopping is a glaring example of how the digital age has changed the way consumers and businesses interact. Companies have to adjust to the new normal of online buying or risk losing customers.

Key developments in the world of online shopping and marketplaces:

a. Omnichannel Retail: Companies are combining online and offline channels to make buying easier for customers. The convenience of online shopping with in-store pickup is now offered by even the largest shops like Walmart.

b. Dominance of the Market: E-commerce giants like Amazon and Alibaba have taken a sizable portion of the market, making it necessary for brick-and-mortar stores to either compete with or develop strategic alliances with these platforms to reach a larger client base.

c. Direct-to-Consumer (DTC) Brands: Digital natives like Warby Parker and Casper have disrupted conventional sectors by selling directly to customers online, bypassing middlemen and driving down prices.

3. Decisions Based on Data

Data has been called "the new oil" of the digital age. In order to better their operations, businesses are collecting massive volumes of data and using analytics software to draw conclusions.

The importance of data in organisational change:

a. Personalization: Businesses are utilising client information to provide individualised service. Content recommendation is where streaming services like Netflix really shine.

Forecasting demand, optimising prices, and managing inventory more efficiently are all possible thanks to b. Predictive Analytics, which makes use of predictive models and machine learning algorithms.

c. Customer Insights: The data gleaned from social media and web analytics can be used to fine-tune a company's offerings and advertising tactics in response to what its customers are saying.

4. Working from Home with Cloud Services

Cloud computing has revolutionised the way in which corporations handle their IT needs and facilitate telecommuting. Traditional on-premises solutions lack the scalability, adaptability, and efficiency that cloud services give.

How cloud computing is changing the way businesses function

a. Scalability: Businesses may easily increase or decrease their IT resources to meet fluctuating demand.

The cloud has made it possible for an unprecedented number of people to work remotely. The COVID-19 pandemic prompted many businesses to adopt remote work strategies, with employees relying on cloud-based communication technologies like Zoom and Microsoft Teams to get their jobs done.

c. Money Saved: By using cloud services, organisations no longer have to buy and maintain costly hardware and data centres.

5. Difficulties in Cybersecurity

Despite the many positive effects of the digital era, it has also opened up new dangers for organisations, most notably in the field of cybersecurity. Cybercriminals see a growing opportunity in targeting businesses as they increasingly rely on digital technologies.

Cybersecurity's Challenges and Solutions:

a. Data Breaches: Businesses must invest heavily in cybersecurity measures to safeguard private consumer and company information from being compromised. Encryption, frequent security audits, and educated workers all fall under this category.

Training and awareness programmes for employees are crucial in reducing the dangers posed by phishing assaults. b. Phishing and Social Engineering.

c. Compliance and Regulation: Companies must negotiate a tangled web of data protection laws, such as the European Union's

General Data Protection Regulation (GDPR) and California's Consumer Privacy Act (CCPA). Maintaining legal compliance is important, but doing the right thing by your consumers is even more important.

Sixthly, The Value of Online Advertising

This is especially true of marketing in the digital age. Businesses today need to redirect their marketing efforts and resources into the digital sphere because traditional advertising approaches are no longer productive.

The Digital Marketing Strategies that companies are using nowadays are:

Social media advertising: Facebook, Instagram, and Twitter all have advertising possibilities that can be narrowed down to a specific audience.

b. Content Marketing: By consistently publishing high-quality articles, organisations can build trust as an industry leader and see an increase in organic search engine traffic.

c. Influencer Marketing: Working with popular figures on social media allows brands to obtain exposure and reputation within the influencers' fan bases.

7. Automation and Artificial Intelligence

Artificial intelligence (AI) and automation are transforming businesses by doing formerly human-only jobs more effectively and with fewer mistakes than ever before.

Business uses for artificial intelligence and robotics:

a. Customer Service: Chatbots and virtual assistants offer instantaneous support, addressing frequently asked inquiries and resolving issues for customers around the clock.

b. Data Analysis: AI algorithms are able to quickly evaluate large datasets, allowing them to spot patterns and trends that people would overlook.

c. Manufacturing and Robotics: Manufacturing heavily utilises automation to boost output while simultaneously decreasing labour expenses.

Sustainability and Business Ethics 8.

Sustainability and business responsibility are receiving more attention in the modern day. More and more customers are thinking twice about the companies they buy from because of their potential negative effects on society and the environment.

Sustainability actions being taken by businesses:

a. Lowering Carbon Footprint: Businesses are embracing sustainable methods such as switching to renewable energy, cutting down on waste, and installing energy-saving equipment.

b. Social Responsibility: Corporations are actively engaging in social causes and philanthropy, thereby associating their names with beliefs held by their target markets.

c. Transparency: Transparency in corporate practises is becoming more crucial to build consumer trust, especially in regards to sourcing and supply chains.

Adjusting to a Changing World 9.

The advent of the digital age has hastened globalisation, making it simpler for companies to expand into other markets. However, there are possibilities and threats in responding to global competition and varying consumer tastes.

Methods of adjusting to a globalised world:

a. Localization: modifying goods and services as well as advertising campaigns to meet the language and cultural demands of target markets

.

b. E-commerce Exporting: By selling goods online and taking use of international shipping services, small enterprises can reach a global client base.

The obstacles of breaking into new markets can be mitigated by the formation of global partnerships.

10. The Digital Age and the Future of Business

Anticipating future trends and maintaining flexibility is crucial for organisations as they continue to adjust to the digital age. The commercial world will continue to be moulded by cutting-edge innovations such as blockchain, quantum computing, and 5G.

What the future holds for companies in the information age:

a. Blockchain Technology: Blockchain has the ability to radically alter logistics, security, and monetary exchanges.

b. 5G Connectivity: New applications and services, especially in the Internet of Things (IoT) and augmented reality (AR) fields, will be made possible by faster and more reliable 5G networks.

c. Quantum Computing: Quantum computing has the potential to revolutionise industries like cryptography and materials science by solving complicated problems at rates currently impossible with conventional computers.

In conclusion, companies in the modern digital era are doing more than just adjusting to the changes brought on by the Internet. In today's competitive corporate environment, digital transformation is no longer a luxury but a must. Companies that want to succeed in the digital age must be nimble, creative, and customer-focused as technology undergoes constant change. The leaders of tomorrow's digital business world will be those who understand how to leverage digital technologies while also tackling issues of security, sustainability, and globalisation.

2.2- Case studies of successful digital transformations

Examples of Effective Digital Transitions

A strategic imperative in today's ever-changing corporate environment, digital transformation is more than simply a buzzword. Digital technologies are being used by businesses across all sectors to revamp their core operations, provide better service to customers, and boost expansion. To learn how organisations have adapted to the digital age, we will analyse numerous real-world instances of successful digital transformations in this case study inquiry.

Amazon.com: First a Bookseller, Now a Retail Powerhouse1

It's not just survived, but prospered, in the face of digital disruption; Amazon is a prime example. What began in the 1990s as an online bookstore has grown into the largest e-commerce platform in the world.

- Digital Innovation: Amazon upended the retail industry with innovations such as one-click buying, customised suggestions, and the Amazon Prime membership programme, which offers free two-day shipping and access to a library of online videos.

Data-driven decision making: Amazon's algorithms leverage customer behaviour and purchase history to personalise product recommendations, enhancing the shopping experience and ultimately driving more business.

Amazon Web Services (AWS) has become a frontrunner in the cloud computing industry by delivering highly scalable and reasonably priced infrastructure services to companies all over the world.

Amazon has made investments in robotic automation and advanced supply chain management technologies to optimise its supply chain and speed up the fulfilment and delivery of customer orders.

Netflix Is Changing the Face of Entertainment for the Better

Netflix was just a DVD rental service, but thanks to its adoption of digital technologies, it has now evolved into a global streaming behemoth, revolutionising the entertainment industry.

Netflix has put a lot of resources into creating original content by employing data analytics to figure out what its customers want to see. Shows like "Stranger Things" and "House of Cards" demonstrate their winning approach to content creation.

Netflix's recommendation algorithm takes into account user preferences, viewing history, and ratings to create a unique homepage for each member, which has been shown to increase both engagement and retention.

Netflix's rapid growth and international expansion to serve millions of customers in dozens of countries is a direct result of the company's early adoption of digital distribution.

Third, Tesla: Disrupting the Automobile Market.

Tesla's introduction of electric vehicles (EVs) and advancements in autonomous driving technology shook up the automobile market.

Tesla's electric cars have reshaped the industry by providing eco-friendly, high-performance alternatives to conventional gas-powered automobiles.

By leveraging digital technology, Tesla is able to provide over-the-air software updates that improve the functionality, security, and overall performance of the vehicle. Thanks to this feature, Tesla vehicles are always evolving to become better.

- Autonomous Driving: Tesla's Autopilot and Full Self-Driving technologies are at the forefront of autonomous car technology, solidifying the brand's position as an industry pioneer.

Quick-Service Restaurant Leader McDonald's Embraces Digital Innovation

For better service to customers and more efficient business practises, McDonald's has gone through a digital transformation.

- Digital Ordering: McDonald's now offers more ways to place an order digitally, including digital ordering kiosks, mobile apps, and delivery services.

The organisation employs data analytics to learn about its clients' tastes so it can better cater to them. Customers can, for instance, use the "Create Your Taste" interface to personalise their burgers.

McDonald's uses digital technology to improve supply chain management, which in turn guarantees that its restaurants throughout the world always have access to fresh supplies.

5. Walmart: Merging the In-Store and Online Experiences

The massive retail chain Walmart has effectively combined online and physical shopping.

To further expand into the e-commerce business, Walmart purchased the online marketplace Jet.com. The corporation has expanded its online offerings to compete with Amazon.

Walmart's in-store technology includes automatic shelf-scanning robots, RFID inventory tracking, and self-service checkout kiosks.

Walmart has invested in a digitally connected supply chain, which allows for real-time inventory tracking and enhanced product availability.

Sixthly, Digital Transformation at Starbucks:

To better serve its customers and encourage brand loyalty, Starbucks has embraced digital change.

Customers can now order ahead, pay via their phones and escape the queue at Starbucks thanks to the company's new mobile ordering and payment feature, available via the company's app.

- Customer Engagement: By rewarding repeat customers, Starbucks encourages customer loyalty and leverages customer information to tailor offers and suggestions.

- In-shop Digital Innovation: Starbucks stores now have digital menu boards that customers can interact with, and the company also makes use of other digital tools to improve things like inventory management and shop efficiency.

7 Airbnb: Revolutionising the Hotel Business

By facilitating connections between hosts and guests, Airbnb has shaken up the traditional hotel business.

Airbnb's online platform serves as a marketplace where hosts may post listings for available rooms and guests can book those rooms, thereby establishing a global community of hosts and guests.

- Community and Trust: Airbnb users feel more connected to one another since they can trust the reviews and ratings other users have left.

Airbnb is able to rapidly enter new markets and provide a wide variety of lodging options because to the digital technology that supports this expansion.

Bank of America is Bringing Financial Services into the 21st Century.

In an effort to bring its banking services up to date, Bank of America has begun a journey of digital transformation.

The bank has created mobile banking apps, so users can do things like cheque deposits and account maintenance from the convenience of their own cellphones using the bank's Digital Banking system.

- Artificial Intelligence (AI) Powered Assistants: Bank of America developed Erica, an AI-powered virtual assistant, to assist customers with financial activities and deliver tailored advice.

Biometric authentication is only one example of how digital technology is improving security to keep sensitive client information safe.

These examples show how businesses in various fields have adapted to the Internet age. They show how digital transformation may be used to create new business models, better serve existing customers, and gain a competitive edge. Data-driven decision making, consumer personalisation, international expansion, and the incorporation of digital technology into core operations are common threads running through these success stories. These models can act as motivation for companies in the modern era of digital disruption and technical advancement.

2.3- Emerging technologies and their role in business growth

The Impact of New Technology on Company Expansion

The way businesses function, compete, and expand is being revolutionised by new technologies in today's ever-changing technological landscape. These ground-breaking developments have the potential to radically alter existing business models, boost productivity, and open up entirely new markets. Examining the trends, possibilities, and challenges that businesses confront as they adopt new technologies, this investigation will delve into the profound effect that emerging technologies are having on their development and expansion.

One, Machine Learning and Artificial Intelligence (AI)

AI and ML are cutting-edge innovations that provide businesses with potent resources for improving decision-making, automating processes, and deriving insights from data.

- Improved User Satisfaction and Engagement thanks to AI-powered chatbots and virtual assistants' individualised customer care.

- Predictive Analytics: Machine learning algorithms examine large datasets to make educated guesses about customer behaviour, supply chain optimisation, and demand forecasting; these actions lead to savings and revenue growth.

- Product Recommendations: E-commerce platforms use AI to make suggestions to customers about what they might want to buy based on their previous searches and purchases.

Second, the IoT (Internet of Things.

The term "Internet of Things" is used to describe a system of networked computing devices, sensors, and other items that may share and exchange data. More and more companies are using IoT to keep tabs on their assets, automate processes, and improve decision-making.

Improve inventory management and cut down on losses with real-time asset tracking made possible by Internet of Things (IoT) sensors.

With the use of Internet of Things (IoT) data, businesses can foresee when repair on their equipment will be required, allowing them to save money by avoiding unscheduled downtime.

In Industry 4.0, where smart factories use information gathered from their networked machinery to enhance their output, the Internet of Things plays a vital role.

Third, the Blockchain

Transactions and records can be kept openly and safely with the use of blockchain technology. Despite its strong association with the cryptocurrency industry, its usefulness extends to many others.

- Supply Chain Transparency: Blockchain technology provides an immutable ledger that documents the origin and distribution of goods.

- Smart Contracts: Businesses can use blockchain-based smart contracts to automate contract execution and payments, cutting down on paperwork and saving time and money.

Secure and verifiable digital identities are made possible by Blockchain technology, which helps to reduce fraud and improve online security.

Fourth, 5G Networking

The introduction of 5G networks is expected to dramatically improve online interaction. The Internet of Things (IoT), augmented reality (AR), and driverless vehicles are just a few of the many uses for this lightning-fast, lag-free technology.

Faster and more dependable mobile connectivity is made possible by 5G, leading to an enhanced mobile experience for both consumers and enterprises.

The low latency of 5G makes it ideal for edge computing, which processes and analyses data in real time at or near its source.

5G is crucial for the creation and maintenance of autonomous vehicles because it enables seamless, in-the-moment data transfer and navigation.

Computing on the Quantum Level

When it comes to computer power, quantum computing is a game-changer. Quantum computing, however still in its infancy, has the ability to solve complex problems that classical computers could not.

Quantum computers can process and analyse large datasets at rates beyond the capabilities of classical computers; this has important implications for fields such as science, finance, and medicine.

There is a pressing need for quantum-resistant encryption solutions because quantum computing presents a threat to existing cryptographic systems.

Sixthly, we have augmented and virtual realities.

Immersive experiences are made possible by augmented and virtual reality technology, which have many uses beyond the entertainment and education sectors.

Businesses can utilise augmented reality to improve the online shopping experience by providing virtual try-on services for clothing and accessories.

- Training and Simulation: Virtual reality is used for training and simulation, offering a risk-free and inexpensive solution for workers to practise difficult tasks in a controlled environment.

- Medical Diagnosis and Treatment: Augmented and virtual reality are used in the medical field for imaging, surgery planning, and patient education.

7. Bioengineering and genetic manipulation

Biomedical services, agricultural production, and the pharmaceutical industry can all benefit greatly from recent developments in biotechnology and genetic engineering.

Insights into an individual's genetic make-up allow for personalised medicine, which boosts treatment efficacy and decreases adverse effects by adapting care to each patient's unique DNA.

Genetically modified crops have higher yields, are more resistant to pests, and help create a more sustainable agricultural system.

Biotechnology speeds up the research and development of new medicines, leading to ground-breaking therapies for a wide range of ailments.

Technology Eighth: Robotics and Automaton

Improvements in production, shipping, and even customer service are being driven by robotics and automation technologies.

Robots and automation systems can increase output and decrease expenses by precisely carrying out repetitive and labor-intensive tasks.

Supply chain effectiveness is enhanced by the deployment of autonomous robots in the aforementioned logistics and warehousing sector.

Chatbots powered by artificial intelligence (AI) are being used in customer service to do mundane chores so that humans may focus on more intricate issues.

Issues and Things to Think About

While new technologies present exciting opportunities for expansion, businesses also face a number of obstacles.

- Data Privacy and Security: As organisations acquire and use more customer data, they must make protecting that data a top priority in order to keep customers' trust and meet the requirements of laws like GDPR.

- Talent Shortages: The developing technology fields are suffering from a lack of qualified personnel due to the rapid speed of technological change. Training and talent acquisition are areas where businesses must spend money.

- Compliance with Regulations: Regulatory frameworks typically lag behind technological advancements. To prevent legal and compliance difficulties, businesses must keep up with the ever-changing regulatory landscape.

- Costs and Return on Investment: New technology adoption can be pricey. Businesses need a solid business case for adoption, which includes a thorough analysis of the potential returns.

Conclusion

New technologies are essential to the expansion and reinvention of businesses of all stripes. From artificial intelligence and the internet of things to blockchain and 5G, these innovations provide companies with fresh opportunities to delight customers, streamline processes, and gain a competitive edge. However, in order to successfully implement, businesses must tackle issues including data security, talent acquisition, regulatory compliance, and cost management. If you want your company to succeed in the digital age, you need to be one of the first to adopt new technologies and strategically use them.

Chapter 3:
The Effects of New Technologies on Society

3.1- Social media's influence on communication and relationships

The Impact of Social Media on Human Interaction

The proliferation of social media has drastically altered the ways in which we interact with one another. Social media has changed the way we live our lives by facilitating communication, spreading news and information, and building and maintaining relationships with people all over the world. In this investigation, we will look into the enormous effect that social media has had on interpersonal interaction, examining its benefits and drawbacks in the context of the modern digital era.

(1) Greater Global Access and Interoperability

By facilitating instantaneous connection over great distances, social media platforms have dramatically altered the nature of human interaction. People from all around the world can interact with one another on social media sites like Facebook, Twitter, Instagram, and LinkedIn. This widespread accessibility has promoted cross-cultural understanding and acceptance by lowering communication barriers and increasing people's awareness of their shared humanity.

- Cultural Exchange: People can learn about and appreciate other people's customs, beliefs, and ways of life through the use of social media, which fosters an atmosphere of acceptance and understanding.

To raise awareness and rally support for causes all across the world, activists have turned to social media, which has played a crucial part in recent political and social revolutions.

Second, the ability to communicate and share data in real time

The ability to instantly disseminate and discuss information is a major benefit of social media platforms. Public opinion and the themes being discussed are influenced by the rapid dissemination of news, events, and personal updates.

- Dissemination of News: Many people rely on social media as their main source of news since it allows them to stay up-to-date on world events in real time and facilitates debate on topical issues.

Ideas, humour, and creative content can spread swiftly throughout the internet thanks to the proliferation of viral trends, memes, and challenges on social media platforms.

3. Fortifying Existing Relationships

The way we keep in touch with friends and family has been revolutionised by social media, which allows us to do so despite physical distances. Social media sites like Facebook make it easy for people to keep tabs on one another's lives by posting updates, images, and messages.

- Virtual Gatherings: Social media platforms allow for virtual gatherings, bringing people together from all over the world to celebrate birthdays, holidays, and other important occasions despite physical distance.

- Support Networks: Social media communities and support groups help people feel less alone by bringing together people who are going through similar experiences and sharing their stories and insights.

Fourthly, how it affects couples' love lives.

The nature of romantic relationships have also been altered by the rise of social media, which has provided novel opportunities for making and maintaining romantic connections and expressing love feelings.

- Online Dating: Dating apps and websites have revolutionised the dating scene by facilitating connections between people who share common interests and preferences.

- Public Displays of Affection: Social media platforms offer outlets for couples to share public displays of affection by posting images, messages, and updates about their relationships to their respective networks.

5. Obstacles and Dangers

While there are many positives to using social media, there are also drawbacks that can hinder communication and cause strain in relationships.

Addiction to digital media can have negative effects on a person's ability to focus, get work done, and interact with others in the real world.

Constantly being exposed to well curated content on social media platforms can lead to social comparison, in which users compare their own lives to those of their peers, which can lead to feelings of inadequacy and low self-esteem.

Cyberbullying is a sort of online harassment that has real-world consequences, including physical and mental health problems for those who are targeted.

Concerns regarding privacy, data security, and the possible exploitation of personal data are raised by the extensive disclosure of private information on social networking platforms.

Conclusion

The impact of social media on people's ability to connect with one another and express themselves is evident. It has revolutionised the way we talk to one another, opening doors to people all over the world, letting them share information in real time, and cementing bonds between individuals. But it's important for people to do so with caution, keeping in mind the potential risks that come with using social media.

Individuals can make the most of social media to improve their communication and foster meaningful relationships if they approach it thoughtfully, with an emphasis on empathy, respect, and privacy. Maintaining the positive effects of social media while mitigating its negative aspects is essential if we want to keep enjoying their benefits in the digital age. To a large extent, the future of communication and the dynamics of human interactions will be determined by how well people utilise social media responsibly.

3.2- Digital activism and its role in shaping society

The Impact of Online Movements on Culture and Society

A new era of activism has emerged with the rise of the internet, in which people use online resources to lobby for political and social reform. Digital activism, often known as online activism, is a growing social movement with significant societal impact. Our investigation will delve into the inner workings of digital activism, looking at its strategies, outcomes, and the ways in which it has altered more conventional forms of advocacy and civic engagement.

(1) Giving People a Voice and Boosting Their Causes

By providing a platform for individuals and underrepresented groups to express their concerns, tell their stories, and fight for their rights, digital activism has democratised the lobbying process. The internet's social media, blogs, and forums give individuals a place to voice their ideas and rally others to action on a wide range of issues.

- Amplification of Marginalised Voices: Digital platforms have provided a voice for marginalised communities that have been underrepresented or silenced in mainstream media.

- Global Solidarity: Through online action, people from all over the world are able to show support for one another and form global movements to combat systematic injustices and advance human rights.

(2) Grassroots organising and communication

By streamlining activist outreach, action planning, and connection with like-minded individuals, digital platforms have revolutionised grass-roots organising.

- Crowdsourcing and Fundraising: Activists can crowdfund their projects and campaigns using online platforms, receiving monetary contributions from people all over the world.

Digital communication allows for speedy organisational responses to social and political developments. Protests, campaigns, and petitions can be quickly organised in reaction to new issues by activists.

Thirdly, the transformative power of social media.

The widespread and easily available nature of social media makes it an integral part of digital activism by offering a forum for spreading information, rallying support, and calling decision-makers to account.

Hashtags on social media sites like Twitter and Instagram have become potent emblems of social movements, serving to unite people behind common causes and spark discussion in the public sphere.

Awareness campaigns, videos, and infographics can quickly spread through social media platforms, informing the public about important social concerns and sparking conversations about how to change the status quo.

Fourthly, Influence and Responsibility in Politics

Citizens are now better able to participate in political processes, hold their representatives responsible, and lobby for policy changes because to the rise of digital activism, which has changed the political landscape.

- Online Petitioning and Advocacy: Websites like Change.org make it possible for people to start and sign petitions, allowing them to have their voices heard and putting pressure on authorities to address their concerns.

Digital platforms enable whistleblowers and activists to reveal corruption and misbehaviour, which can then lead to investigations and prosecutions of those responsible.

5. Obstacles and Moral Concerns

Although digital activism has resulted in many positive improvements, it also raises important problems and ethical questions that must be answered.

- Online Harassment: Harassment and threats against activists, especially women and members of marginalised communities, are a major deterrent to their engagement in digital activism.

- Algorithmic Bias: Social media algorithms can reinforce prejudices, causing echo chambers in which users are only exposed to content that confirms their preexisting ideas.

Because governments and companies may monitor internet activities, endangering individuals' safety, activists must deal with concerns about data security and privacy.

Conclusion

The rise of online activism has significantly altered people's approach to social and political concerns. Digital activism has enabled individuals and groups to fight injustice, demand accountability, and create positive change by offering a forum for marginalised voices, facilitating grassroots mobilisation, and creating global solidarity.

Promoting digital literacy, ethical online behaviour, and diversity, however, is vital for society to fully exploit the potential of digital activism and overcome its difficulties. Digital activism may continue to be a potent force for creating a more just, equitable, and democratic society if people are equipped with the knowledge and skills necessary to critically engage with digital platforms.

In order to create a strong civil society in which everyone's voice is heard and respected, regardless of their background or beliefs, it will be crucial in the future to take use of the possibilities presented by digital activism while addressing its limits. The growth of online activism and its impact on social and political movements make it a crucial factor in determining our society's destiny.

3.3- Ethical considerations in the digital age

Moral Issues in the Information Age

The enormous technological breakthroughs of the digital age have changed practically every facet of human life, from the ways in which we communicate and gain access to information to the ways in which we run our businesses and connect with others. These technology advancements have made many things easier and more convenient, but they have also given rise to a number of ethical concerns that need serious thought and active management. In this investigation, we will delve into the murky waters of the digital age's ethics by looking at the most pressing problems and potential solutions.

One, Securing Personal Information

Significant worries regarding data privacy and security have been voiced in relation to the acquisition and use of personal data in the digital era. Organisations should make ethical data management a top priority, as individuals are more likely to provide personal information online.

- Informed Consent: Ethical Data Practises entail getting informed consent from individuals before collecting their data, explicitly stating how the data will be used, and offering users the option to opt in or out.

- Data Breaches: Companies have a moral obligation to keep their customers' information safe from hackers. In the event of a breach, it is crucial to immediately notify those affected and take corrective measures.

- Transparency: Users' trust can be bolstered by openness about how their data is collected and used. Companies should offer transparent and straightforward privacy practises.

Inequality in the Digital Age

The digital age has widened preexisting gaps in people's access to resources. To ensure that all people have equal access and opportunity in the digital age, it is morally required that the digital divide be closed.

The term "Digital Inclusion" refers to the effort made by governments, organisations, and communities to guarantee that marginalised and underserved groups have access to the internet and other forms of digital technology.

Education and training in digital skills are essential if people are to be able to fully benefit from the digital economy.

Thirdly, Cyberbullying and Online Harassment

Online harassment and cyberbullying are on the rise due to the anonymity and accessibility of the internet, and they can have devastating effects on victims.

Protecting users from harassment, abuse, and threats should be a top priority for all platforms and online communities.

- Digital Citizenship Education: Teaching people how to be safe, respectful, and responsible online can reduce incidents of cyberbullying.

4. Prejudice and bias in artificial intelligence

Concerns concerning bias and fairness in algorithmic decision making have increased as the use of AI systems increases. Discrimination and inequality can be reinforced by algorithms with bias.

Organisations that place a premium on ethics should perform regular audits of their AI systems in order to root out and correct any bias that may exist in the underlying data or coding.

By encouraging a more diverse set of minds to work on AI's development, bias can be mitigated and more perspectives can be taken into account during the design phase.

5. False and misleading information spread via the internet

Significant ethical difficulties are posed by the rapid dissemination of fake news, deception, and misinformation online, which undermines trust in information sources and the political process.

- Media Literacy: Educating people on how to evaluate information and separate fact from fiction is crucial if they are to make educated choices.

The dissemination of accurate information is essential in the fight against misinformation, and this is where fact-checking and verification organisations come in.

Sixth: Digital Dependence

A person's mental health, productivity, and relationships can all take a hit if they spend too much time glued to a screen.

Individuals and families can benefit from a "digital detox" by limiting their screen time and increasing their participation in offline activities.

Companies in the IT industry can help reduce the prevalence of digital addiction by adhering to responsible design principles.

7. Invasion of Privacy Through Surveillance

Ethical concerns regarding bulk data gathering and privacy infringement have been expressed in response to government and corporate surveillance, which is sometimes justified in the name of national security or marketing.

Ethical reasons require that governments maintain civil rights, including the right to privacy, and that businesses safeguard customer information.

- Regulatory Frameworks: Strong privacy and surveillance legislation are crucial to protecting individual rights and must be developed and enforced.

8. Copyright and Intellectual Property

Copyright infringement and IP rights have become more contentious issues in the digital era due to the ease with which intellectual property may be copied, shared, and distributed.

Ethical content creators and consumers will adhere to copyright laws and properly attribute works while making use of them.

Creative Commons licences allow for the safe distribution and reuse of works created by others while also protecting the rights of those who made them.

9. Robotics and the Threat of Job Loss

Concerns about job loss and the moral obligation to retrain affected workers have arisen in response to the widespread adoption of automation and AI.

Organisations should fund reskilling and upskilling initiatives to better prepare their workforces for the future of work.

To help those who may lose their jobs as a result of automation, governments should set up social safety nets.

Tenth, the effect on the environment

There has been an increase in e-waste and energy consumption due to the rapid growth in the number of digital devices and data centres.

Ethical businesses can take steps to reduce their impact on the environment by implementing sustainable practises like recycling and using energy-saving technologies.

To lessen the environmental toll of the information age, it's important to encourage the creation of eco-friendly products and technologies.

Conclusion

Many new ethical concerns have emerged in the digital age, requiring attention and action from individuals, groups, and policymakers. These ethical challenges, which range from data privacy and security to digital inequality and the effects of automation, are inextricably linked to the lightning-fast development of new technologies.

Transparency, fairness, respect for privacy, and a determination to close the digital divide are all ideals that must be upheld if one is to successfully navigate the digital age's ethical landscape. To make sure the digital age is a force for good while protecting people's rights and communities' well-being, there needs to be constant discussion about the ethical questions it raises and strong ethical frameworks and policies put in place. We can create a more just and accountable digital future if we approach these problems with a commitment to ethics.

Chapter 4:
Learning and Technology in the Classroom

4.1- The digitalization of education and e-learning platforms

The Rise of Online Courses and the Internet's Impact on Schooling

Learning and teaching have been revolutionised by the widespread availability of digital resources and online courses. As a result of technological advancements, the classroom as we know it is no longer necessary, and we are entering a new era of digital education. In this investigation, we will look into the changes brought about by the digitization of education, analysing the primary motivators, advantages, disadvantages, and forthcoming tendencies that are influencing the way we teach and learn today.

The Digital Transformation of Learning: Influential Factors

There is a perfect storm of forces propelling the widespread adoption and development of education's digital transformation:

Access to digital education has been facilitated by technological advancements such as the widespread availability of high-speed internet, the accessibility of affordable computer equipment, and the creation of sophisticated software.

Access to knowledge from all over the world is made possible by the worldwide web, which has broken down geographical barriers between students and teachers.

- Content Customization and Individualization: With today's digital tools, students can have lessons designed just for their interests and learning styles.

To emphasise the significance of digitalization in education, consider the following: - Remote Learning Necessity: Events like the COVID-19 pandemic pushed the acceptance of e-learning as a vital means of remote education.

The advantages of online learning

There are many ways in which the digitization of education benefits both students and teachers:

Digital education removes geographical and socioeconomic constraints, making it available to people of all ages and walks of life.

Working professionals and non-traditional students can fit education into their hectic schedules thanks to the portability and adaptability offered by e-learning systems.

- Cost-Efficiency: Compared to traditional textbooks and classroom materials, digital resources can be more cost-effective, easing the financial strain on students and educational institutions.

Multimedia, quizzes, simulations, and gamified content are common features of digital education, all of which increase student engagement and retention.

- Insights Fueled by Data: Because of the data collected by e-learning systems, teachers can better personalise lessons, pinpoint problem areas, and monitor students' growth.

Thirdly, Issues to Think About

Despite the enormous potential, digital education also poses obstacles and issues that must be addressed if it is to fulfil that promise.

- Digital Divide: Some pupils have less access to computers and the internet than others, putting them at a disadvantage. Equal educational opportunity requires closing the digital divide.

The proliferation of online resources means that vetting them for truth and reliability is more difficult than ever.

Institutions of higher learning have a special responsibility to ensure the confidentiality of student records.

Teachers may need training in the proper use of digital resources before they can incorporate them into their classrooms effectively.

- Engagement and Motivation: With the possibility for distractions and isolation, it can be difficult to keep students interested and motivated in online learning environments.

(4) Varieties of Online Courseware

Different types of e-learning platforms are designed for different audiences and purposes.

- Learning Management Systems (LMS): LMS platforms like Moodle and Blackboard serve as a one-stop shop for all things related to a certain class, including materials, tests, and discussions.

- Massive Open Online Courses (MOOCs): MOOC platforms like Coursera, edX, and Udacity make high-quality courses from universities and other institutions available to a wide audience for free or at a low cost.

Different people have different learning styles, therefore e-learning can be either synchronous (real-time engagement) or asynchronous (self-paced).

Many companies now use e-learning systems like LinkedIn Learning and Skillsoft to provide ongoing education and training for their staff members.

Apps like Duolingo and Rosetta Stone, which provide gamified and interactive language-learning experiences, have revolutionised the field.

5. The Prospects for Online Learning in the Long Run

Several new developments are shaping the future of education in the digital age, including:

Personalised learning recommendations, automated evaluations, and intelligent tutoring systems are all possible thanks to AI-powered technologies in the classroom, and to the use of AI.

- Augmented and Virtual Reality (AR/VR): AR and VR technologies provide immersive learning experiences, especially in areas like medical education, engineering, and simulations.

Microlearning, in which information is broken down into manageable chunks and presented in a series of short, self-contained modules, is becoming increasingly popular.

To improve the trustworthiness and accessibility of academic credentials, blockchain technology can be used to securely verify and exchange them.

To better engage and inspire students, educators are increasingly turning to the fields of Gamification and Edutainment.

Conclusion

E-learning platforms and the general trend towards digitising the educational process have brought about a sea change in how we learn new things. This shift has democratised the educational system by making it more adaptable, accessible, and individual. But there are problems with accessibility, quality, and participation that need to be addressed.

The future of online learning looks bright because of the exponential growth of computing power. Artificial intelligence (AI), augmented reality (AR/VR), microlearning, and blockchain have the potential to significantly improve education. It is essential for schools, governments, and other stakeholders to work together to overcome obstacles and make the most of digital education's many advantages. Doing so will allow us to maintain our progress towards universal secondary education and equip individuals with the tools they need to succeed in the knowledge-based economies that will define the 21st century.

4.2- Online education's benefits and drawbacks

There are pros and cons to online learning.

E-learning, or online education, has become a game-changer in the educational system, altering the way students study and retain information. Due to the proliferation of digital technologies and online resources, people can now study from the convenience of their own homes or from any other location with an internet connection. There are many upsides to online learning, but it also has its cons and difficulties. To fully comprehend the shifting educational landscape, we will examine the benefits and drawbacks of online learning in this investigation.

Advantages of Distance Learning

1) Accessibility and Flexibility: Online education has made education available to more people, regardless of their location or physical ability. Students can study and take part in classes whenever and wherever they have internet access.

Second, the Internet is a rich resource for learning about a wide variety of topics and developing skillsets. Students have access to a wide range of subjects, from the general to the highly specialised.

3. Cost-Effective: Students can save money on tuition, transportation, and living expenses by taking classes online. Because of this, more people will be able to get the education they need.

Individualised course plans are made possible by the flexibility of digital learning environments. Students can design their own learning paths according to their specific interests and career objectives by picking and choosing from various courses, modules, and micro-credentials.

5. A World View: Students in an online class may come from all over the world and have a wide range of experiences and perspectives to share. This world view enhances conversations and fosters mutual appreciation for other cultures.

Many online courses are self-paced, so students can work through the content at their own pace. This adaptability is helpful for students with a wide range of needs and schedules.

7. Improved Technology Integration: Online learning makes use of cutting-edge tools to present interesting and engaging material. The use of multimedia tools like quizzes, simulations, and virtual labs can greatly benefit the educational process.

Disadvantages and Difficulties of Online Learning

One of the biggest problems with online learning is that there is no face-to-face contact between students and teachers. Real-time conversations, peer-to-peer cooperation, and direct connection with instructors are hallmarks of the traditional classroom setting and can be difficult to reproduce online.

Second, Limited Social Interaction: Students who take their classes online could miss out on the networking, group projects, and extracurricular activities that are integral parts of a traditional classroom experience. A less enriching educational experience may result from isolation and a lack of socialisation.

Technical Challenges (3): Online education necessitates constant connection to the internet and a certain level of technical expertise. Disruptions to the learning process might occur when technical difficulties arise, such as connection issues or computer breakdowns.

Self-motivation and discipline are crucial for students who study alone online. Without the structure of a traditional classroom, it's easy to put off work or fall behind.

5. Varied Quality: While some online courses and programmes provide a high-quality educational experience, others may be less than rigorous or lack an effective instructional design.

6. Assessment and Cheating: It can be more difficult to ensure the integrity of assessments and avoid cheating in an online setting. Academic honesty can only be preserved through the implementation of rigorous institutional policies.

7. Lack of Accreditation: The value of an online education can be diminished if the delivering institution or programme does not have the requisite accreditation. It is the student's responsibility to investigate and confirm that their chosen programmes are accredited.

Hybrid and Blended Education: Finding Common Ground

Many schools have switched to hybrid or blended learning methods because of the pros and cons of online education. These methods attempt to maximise the benefits of both online and in-person learning by fusing them into a single strategy.

Hybrid learning provides students with the advantages of both face-to-face interaction with teachers and peers and remote access to course materials. Blended learning enhances the traditional classroom experience without completely replacing it by incorporating digital tools and online activities.

Online Learning: The Wave of the Future

Online learning is here to stay and will most likely develop further in response to student demand and technology progress. Several developments stand out as possibilities for the future of online learning:

(1) AI and Personalization: AI will play an increasingly important role in customising educational information for individual students, making recommendations based on their unique needs, and automating clerical work.

Second, Virtual Reality (VR) and Augmented Reality (AR) will allow for realistic simulations for professional training and virtual field trips for more interactive learning.

Third, microlearning will rise in popularity, providing learners with the condensed, immediately useful information they crave.

The acceptance of digital badges and other non-traditional forms of credentialing as proof of skills and abilities is expected to increase in the coming years.

5. Global Collaboration: Online education will stimulate increased international collaboration by allowing students and academic institutions from all over the world to work together on projects and assignments.

As remote work and the gig economy continue to develop, so will the demand for online workforce training and upskilling.

7. Improvements to Accessibility: Future innovations will centre on closing the digital gap and making online education available to underserved people.

In sum, there are several advantages to receiving an education online, including convenience, adaptability, and a wide range of options. However, it also includes difficulties in interpersonal communication, technical issues, and intrinsic drive. The goal of hybrid and blended approaches to education is to

the benefits of both virtual and traditional classrooms.

To ensure that students in the digital age have access to high-quality, interesting, and effective learning opportunities, it will be essential to solve these difficulties and embrace developing trends in online education. A dynamic combination of online and traditional learning could provide students with a varied and flexible educational experience, which could be the future of education.

4.3- The role of AI and virtual reality in education

AI and VR's Importance in the Classroom

Virtual reality (VR) and artificial intelligence (AI) are two game-changing technologies that could radically alter the classroom experience. These innovative resources are revolutionising the educational system by giving students and teachers access to more engaging and tailor-made learning environments. Here, we'll investigate how artificial intelligence (AI) and virtual reality (VR) are changing the face of education by looking at their pros, cons, and potential.

Learning with AI

AI is making great strides in the classroom, particularly in the areas of machine learning and natural language processing. It's improving everything from material delivery to grading to administrative duties in the classroom. Some of the most important functions of AI in the classroom include:

1. Personalised Learning: AI-based systems use student data and past learning habits to design unique courses of study. Students are more likely to be actively involved and have a deeper understanding of the material when it is adapted to their own learning styles and pace.

Students receive immediate feedback and suggestions from AI-powered adaptive learning platforms. Based on a user's performance, these systems tailor the platform's question complexity and make available supplementary materials.

Third, Automated Grading and Feedback: AI algorithms can evaluate assignments and tests rapidly and accurately, giving educators more time to focus on students' individual needs. In addition, AI provides pupils with real-time feedback to assist them absorb the lessons from their failures.

AI can create instructional materials like quizzes, flashcards, and lesson plans, leading to improved content creation. It can also gather relevant information and recommend readings to augment lessons.

Natural Language Processing (NLP) is a branch of artificial intelligence that uses large corpora of text to do tasks like translating sentences and grading essays automatically. The programme gives students constructive criticism on their writing in terms of grammar, style, and overall coherence.

Sixth, Virtual Teaching Assistants: AI-powered chatbots and virtual teaching assistants are accessible round-the-clock to respond to students' inquiries, clarify concepts, and offer course-specific advice.

Advantages of AI for Teaching

- Personalization: AI adapts instructional material to each learner, catering to their unique needs.
- Efficiency: Teachers are able to devote more time to instruction because they don't have to worry about grading and other administrative activities that have been automated.
AI can be used to collect and analyse data on student performance, which can then be used by teachers, school leaders, and policymakers to improve education.
- Accessibility: Tools powered by AI can help students with disabilities by giving them access to supplementary support and specialised content.

Issues and Things to Think About

Concerns about data privacy and security arise from the need to acquire and store personal information about students.

Inequitable distribution of AI-enhanced learning resources has the potential to exacerbate current gaps in schooling.
Teachers may need specific instruction on how to make the most of AI resources in the classroom.
Inadvertently reinforcing biases requires careful design and monitoring of AI algorithms, which raises ethical concerns.

Learning using Virtual Reality

Another game-changing innovation, virtual reality (VR) provides students with interactive, three-dimensional educational environments. Virtual reality (VR) has the potential to make learning more engaging and participatory by moving students to virtual surroundings. Key Functions of Virtual Reality in the Classroom

First, virtual reality (VR) can produce realistic simulations and learning environments that fully submerge pupils in the material. Students can use these environments to learn about and interact with a variety of topics, from historical places and virtual animals to chemistry experiments.

Second, Hands-On Learning is made possible by VR because it enables students to engage with phenomena and items that would otherwise be inaccessible or unsafe. Learning and memory are both improved by this practical application.

Third, Virtual Field travels: VR can take students on travels to locations they'll never be able to visit in real life, from the bottom of the ocean to the furthest reaches of the galaxy.

4. Medical and Healthcare Training: Virtual reality (VR) is incredibly useful in the field of medicine since it allows for the practise of complex operations and the simulation of realistic surgical procedures for both medical students and experts.

5. Language Learning: VR can imitate immersive language contexts, giving pupils the chance to practise language skills in authentic circumstances.

The Advantages of Virtual Reality (VR) in the Classroom

- Engagement: Virtual reality (VR) keeps students interested and makes education fun.
- The immersive aspect of VR increases the likelihood that information will be remembered and comprehended.
- Students can safely conduct experiments and other activities in virtual reality.
- Allowing for a wider range of learning styles and demands, virtual reality (VR) is easily accessible.

Issues and Things to Think About

- Implementing virtual reality (VR) can be pricey due to the high upfront and ongoing costs of hardware, software, and upkeep.
- In order to experience virtual reality, users must have access to specialised hardware and a reliable network.
- High-quality virtual reality (VR) content development takes time and money.
- Some people may get motion sickness from using virtual reality headsets.
- Concerns about students' physical safety while using virtual reality headsets have been raised in traditional classroom settings.

The Role of AI and VR in the Classroom of the Future

As these technologies improve, their use in classrooms is expected to grow. New possibilities and developments include:

1. AI-Driven Personalised Learning: Artificial intelligence will get better at tailoring student experiences, leading to more efficient and effective classrooms.

Second, Hybrid Learning Environments will emerge as a result of the incorporation of AI and VR into traditional classrooms, bringing together the finest of both the virtual and the physical worlds of education.

Thirdly, Global Collaboration can be fostered by using VR to bring together students and teachers from all over the world in virtual classrooms.

Adaptive and meaningful tests will be developed and graded with the help of artificial intelligence (AI).

.

The usage of AI-powered tools to assist students with special needs is expected to grow in the near future. These tools will facilitate the delivery of individualised interventions and modifications to the learning environment.

Using immersive simulations, virtual reality (VR) will be utilised to teach "soft skills" including communication, leadership, and empathy

To sum up, AI and VR have the potential to revolutionise the educational system by making it more adaptable, exciting, and immersive for each individual student. There will always be obstacles and things to think about, but the potential benefits of modern technologies in the classroom are enormous. Artificial intelligence (AI) and virtual reality (VR) have the potential to transform the educational experience for students of all ages as they continue to develop and become more widely available.

Chapter 5:
The Rise of the Digital Health Sector

5.1- Telemedicine and remote healthcare services

Healthcare Delivery Via Telecommunications Technology

Telemedicine, often known as telehealth, is a game-changing method of delivering healthcare that makes use of modern technology to do it remotely. This ground-breaking method eliminates the need for patients to physically see healthcare providers for consultations, diagnoses, and treatment. The introduction of the COVID-19 pandemic hastened the adoption of telemedicine and brought to light the significance of expanding access to healthcare services. The purpose of this investigation is to learn more about telemedicine and other forms of remote healthcare by analysing their pros, cons, and potential impact on the future of healthcare delivery.

Telemedicine's Benefits

1. Accessibility and Convenience: Telemedicine removes barriers to healthcare access for people in all parts of the world, but especially those living in rural or underserved areas. Patients can save time and money by contacting healthcare providers without leaving their homes.

Second, Timely Consultations: Telemedicine provides rapid access to medical experts, ensuring that patients, even in emergency situations, receive timely care. In times of medical emergency, this swiftness can be lifesaving.

The management of long-term conditions is an area where telemedicine shines. Regular virtual checkups, adjusting of medications, and condition monitoring can all be done under the supervision of healthcare providers.

Cost reductions for patients and healthcare systems are another benefit of telemedicine. There won't be any need to budget for gas, parking, or entrance costs. Additionally, healthcare providers may be able to see more patients each day through the use of virtual consultations because of the time savings.

5. Improved Continuity of Care: Telemedicine improves continuity of care by letting doctors check in on patients and make necessary adjustments to their treatment plans remotely. The result is better healthcare that is both unified and comprehensive.

During the COVID-19 pandemic, telemedicine's ability to lessen patients' exposure to infection in hospital settings made it an indispensable tool. It would be possible to treat patients without exposing staff to contagious people.

Issues and Things to Think About

The first restriction of telemedicine is that it cannot replace a full physical examination. In order to properly diagnose some medical disorders, it is essential to schedule an in-person appointment.

To complicate matters further, not all patients have access to the technology required to take part in telemedicine, such as smartphones or high-speed internet.

Thirdly, Data Security and Privacy are of paramount importance while conducting virtual consultations with patients. Strict laws and safeguards must be followed by the healthcare industry at all times.

4. Licencing and State rules: Since telemedicine sometimes entails providing care across state or international borders, there may be

complications with obtaining the necessary licences and complying with state rules.

5. Patient Engagement: It might be difficult to make sure patients are involved in and contributing to their healthcare from a distance. It's possible that some patients will need help making the most of telehealth services.

Insurance and reimbursement policies for telemedicine differ by location and provider. Insurance companies may be reluctant to pay for a patient's telemedicine visits.

Technological and Methodological Advances in Telemedicine

A wide variety of tools and methods can be used in telemedicine, such as:

1. Video Conferencing: Patients and doctors can have face-to-face conversations through real-time video consultations, allowing doctors to visually check patients' ailments.

Second, we have Store-and-Forward, an asynchronous approach that entails accumulating patient information for eventual transmission to a professional for analysis and diagnosis.

Thirdly, Remote Monitoring enables continuous monitoring of chronic illnesses through the use of devices such as wearable fitness trackers, glucose monitors, and blood pressure cuffs that transfer patient data to healthcare practitioners.

Using Telepharmacy, chemists can remotely give medication counselling and management to patients.

5. Mobile Health Apps: Apps and platforms designed specifically for use on smartphones can improve two-way communication between

patients and doctors. Potential functions of such apps include video chatting, instant messaging, and information gathering.

Telemedicine's Bright Future

In the coming years, telemedicine is expected to undergo radical changes and expansions. Its future is being shaped by a number of significant trends and developments:

1) Artificial Intelligence and Data Analytics: AI will play a crucial role in telemedicine, helping with everything from diagnosis to outcome prediction and streamlining administrative procedures.

Improved remote monitoring devices, made possible by developments in wearable technology, will give patients a greater say in their own healthcare.

Third, Telemedicine Specialisation: Healthcare practitioners will offer specialised services in fields like dermatology, mental health, and radiology via telemedicine.

4. Telemedicine Integration: Remote healthcare will be supported by electronic health records (EHRs) and other healthcare information technology (IT) systems, and will be fully integrated into the larger healthcare ecosystem.

5. Legislation and Regulation: Lawmakers will keep changing laws and regulations, as well as reimbursement schemes, to accommodate the growing need for telemedicine.

The sixth innovation, Global Telemedicine, will allow patients to access healthcare from providers in other nations.

In conclusion, the advent of telemedicine and other remote healthcare services has revolutionised the healthcare system by increasing its reach, improving patient satisfaction, and reducing costs. Limitations in physical examinations and technological restrictions exist, but these are projected to be solved with the help of new technologies, stricter rules, and patient participation. One trend that will shape healthcare in the future is telemedicine.

vital role, allowing people to access high-quality care regardless of their location, which in turn leads to better health outcomes and less healthcare inequities.

5.2- Wearable technology and its impact on personal health

The Effect of Wearable Technology on Individual Health

In recent years, wearable technology has become a game-changer for improving people's health and well-being. Often integrated into clothing or worn on the body, these cutting-edge gadgets collect data on a person's health and lifestyle in real time and offer valuable insights. Fitness trackers, smartwatches, and other health monitoring wearables have seen a huge uptick in popularity in recent years, and millions of people now regularly use them. This investigation will dig into the realm of wearable technology, assessing its effects on individual health along with its advantages and disadvantages.

The Health Advantages of Wearable Technology

Health Monitoring : Vital signs including heart rate, blood pressure, and sleep patterns can be tracked constantly via wearable devices. Users gain insight into their health as a whole and can catch problems in the early detection stages using this information.

Fitness Tracking 2: Fitness trackers and smartwatches have functions for monitoring physical activity including counting steps, calculating caloric expenditure, and keeping tabs on how far you've gone. Users are inspired to keep moving and achieve their fitness objectives by reading this data.

Heart Health: Wearables with ECG (electrocardiogram) capability can detect irregular heart rhythms like atrial fibrillation. Finding heart problems early can save lives.

Fourth, Sleep Tracking: a wide variety of wearables can inform you about your sleep's quality, length, and disruptions. Users can better manage their sleep and health thanks to this data.

5. Stress Management: Some wearables include stress monitoring functions, and these applications can help you learn to control your stress through activities like deep breathing and guided meditation.

6. Medication Reminders: Wearables can notify and remind users to take their medications at the times doctors have prescribed.

Motivation and a Sense of success 7 Health Goals and Motivation The gamification of health and fitness through wearable technology enables users to create and achieve health goals, promoting motivation and a sense of success.

8. Remote Monitoring: Wearable devices allow medical professionals to keep tabs on their patients' well-being without physically examining them.

9. issue Alerts: In the event of an accident or health issue, certain wearables offer built-in SOS functions that allow users to call for help or notify emergency contacts.

Providing consumers with meaningful insights based on their health data, wearable apps and platforms enable individuals to make educated choices about their health and wellness.

Issues and Things to Think About

Despite its many advantages, wearable technology also comes with some caveats and things to think about:

Concerns regarding privacy and data security are prompted by the collection and storage of individual health data on wearable devices. A user's confidence in the security of their health data is essential.

Second, the reliability of health data collected by wearable devices varies by device and manufacturer. To ensure accurate results, users should only employ tried-and-true gadgets.

Thirdly, User Engagement: many people buy wearables but may not utilise them regularly. Long-term health advantages can only be achieved through sustained user engagement and motivation.

The process of incorporating information from wearable devices into existing healthcare infrastructure and electronic health records (EHRs) is continuously developing. Seamless integration calls for standardisation and interoperability.

5. Overload of Data: Wearables provide a mountain of information. It's possible that users will have difficulty processing and making sense of all the data available to them.

Wearable technology presents ethical problems about data ownership, permission, and the possibility of discrimination based on health data.

7. Battery Life: Some wearables' limited functionality may be due to their batteries, especially if they need to be charged frequently.

8. Accessibility: Wearable technology may not be readily available or user-friendly for everyone, especially those who are elderly or have physical limitations.

Effects on Health and Medicine

There are many ways in which wearable technology is revolutionising healthcare and wellness:

First, Preventive Health: Wearables encourage individuals to take charge of their health by providing tools for self-monitoring and education.

Continuous health monitoring allows for early detection of health disorders, which may avert more serious conditions and lower healthcare expenses.

Third, Remote Patient Monitoring allows doctors to keep an eye on their patients even when they're not physically in the same room, which has been shown to decrease unnecessary hospitalisations and boost long-term health.

4. Telehealth: Health data collected from wearables can be included into telehealth consultations, allowing for better educated judgements and recommendations to be made by healthcare experts.

5. Insights from Research and Data: The pooled information from wearable devices can shed light on medical research and help in the discovery of new therapies and interventions.

By providing users with feedback and inspiration, wearable technology promotes positive behaviour change that benefits their health and well-being.

Forecasting the Future of Wearable Technology

Several new developments are in the horizon for wearable technology as it continues to advance:

One trend in the smartwatch industry is the increased emphasis on health monitoring through the use of sophisticated sensors and functionalities.

2. Continuous Glucose Monitoring: As technology advances, so are wearables that measure blood glucose levels, which is great news for those with diabetes.

Third, Wearable AI: AI will play a larger role in analysing and interpreting wearable health data, resulting in more precise and individualised insights.

Fourth, Healthcare Partnerships: Companies making wearables are teaming together with hospitals, clinics, and insurance companies to boost patient care and lower costs.

Fifth, Hybrid Devices will rise in popularity; these wearables will integrate the functions of fitness trackers, smartwatches, and health monitors.

Form factors for wearable tech will continue to change, with more and more gadgets becoming embedded in anything from clothing to jewellery to contact lenses.

7. Mental Health Focus: Wearables will increasingly address issues related to mental health, providing tools for dealing with stress and maintaining a healthy emotional state. Wearable technology has advanced greatly in the field of individual health and wellbeing, providing users with invaluable information about their own body and mind. The potential of wearable technology for preventative health, early detection, and remote monitoring is clear, but it faces problems such as privacy and data security. Wearable gadgets already play an important part in empowering people to better manage their health, and this is only expected to increase as technology advances.

5.3- Big data and AI in healthcare diagnostics and treatment

AI and Big Data for Medical Diagnosis and Care

Big data and artificial intelligence (AI) are converging to bring about a revolutionary shift in the healthcare sector. Advanced AI algorithms combined with large and complicated healthcare datasets have ushered in a new era of diagnosis and treatment. As a result of this convergence, healthcare is being delivered better, with better outcomes for patients, and medical diagnosis and treatment are being transformed. In this article, we will examine the use of Big Data and AI in healthcare, including their advantages, disadvantages, and potential in the industry.

Big Data's Impact on Healthcare

Electronic health records (EHRs), medical imaging, genomic data, wearable device data, and many other types of data are all examples of what are collectively referred to as "Big Data" in the healthcare industry. The healthcare industry is already seeing the effects of Big Data in the following ways:

1. Improved Diagnostics: Big Data analytics can reveal concealed patterns and insights in medical information, allowing clinicians to make more precise and faster diagnoses.

Second, Predictive Analytics makes use of Big Data to foresee the occurrence of medical crises such as disease outbreaks, patient readmissions, and problems before they occur.

3. Personalised Medicine: Big Data analysis enables the customization of treatment programmes based on factors unique to each patient, such as their genetic makeup, lifestyle choices, and health background.

4. Drug Discovery: Pharmaceutical companies use Big Data to find new drug candidates, anticipate how patients will react to medications, and find new drugs more quickly.

5. Public Health: Strategies and interventions in public health, such as vaccination programmes and the containment of infectious illnesses, can be informed by the analysis of massive datasets.

The sixth application of big data in healthcare is population health management, wherein vulnerable groups in a community are singled out for special attention so that effective preventative and curative measures can be taken.

Diagnostics and Treatment: Artificial Intelligence's Impact in Healthcare

Harnessing the potential of Big Data in healthcare requires the application of artificial intelligence (AI), an area of computer science devoted to the development of intelligent machines capable of learning and problem-solving. Here are some ways in which AI is changing medical diagnosis and care:

First, Disease Identification: By analysing X-rays, MRIs, and CT scans, AI algorithms can help physicians spot and diagnose conditions including cancer, heart disease, and neurological illness.

Clinical decision support systems powered by artificial intelligence let doctors make more informed decisions about patients' diagnoses and treatments.

Third, Natural Language Processing (NLP) algorithms can improve the precision of diagnosis and treatment regimens by extracting useful information from unstructured clinical notes.

4. Genomic Medicine: AI aids in the analysis of large genomic datasets, allowing for the identification of variants that contribute to disease susceptibility and treatment responses.

5. Drug Development: AI hastens drug research by simulating drug interactions with biological targets, making predictions about how different medications will react to one another, and identifying promising candidates for reusing existing drugs.

In order to maximise therapeutic success while minimising adverse effects, AI algorithms can take patient-specific data into account while designing individualised treatment programmes.

Advantages of Big Data and Artificial Intelligence in Medicine

First, Early Disease Detection: Big Data and AI can find diseases at their earliest, most treatable stages, which might save a lot of lives.

AI-enhanced diagnostics lower the possibility of human error, resulting in more precise diagnoses and care strategies. 2. Improved Accuracy.

Predictive analytics aid healthcare practitioners in allocating resources effectively, decreasing both costs and wait times.

Fourth, Personalised Care: Individualised treatment regimens for each patient improve efficacy and contentment.

5. Research Advancements: The use of Big Data and AI has sped up medical research, leading to new discoveries in the understanding of diseases and the development of effective remedies.

Sixth, Telemedicine and Remote Monitoring: AI helps telemedicine by analysing data from remote patients, allowing for virtual consultations, and keeping tabs on chronic illnesses.

Issues and Things to Think About

While there is much to be gained from combining Big Data and AI in healthcare, there are also some important things to keep in mind:

Privacy of patient information is of paramount importance. Strong security measures are a must for the protection of patient data in the healthcare industry.

Second, Data Quality: For trustworthy AI-driven insights and choices, ensuring the accuracy and quality of healthcare data is crucial.

Thirdly, interoperability: it can be difficult to combine information from various electronic health records and wearable devices. It is essential to reach consensus on interoperability standards.

4. Bias and Fairness: Artificial intelligence systems may amplify biases in healthcare data that already exist in the past. Protecting patients' rights in an AI-driven healthcare system is a top priority.

Regulatory Compliance(5): Healthcare providers and technology firms must traverse complex regulatory frameworks such as HIPAA in the United States and GDPR in Europe.

6. Ethical Considerations: When AI is used to make crucial healthcare choices, such as those involving a patient's end-of-life care or therapy allocation, ethical difficulties arise.

Future of Health Care: Big Data and Artificial Intelligence

Several promising trends and innovations are on the horizon at the convergence of Big Data and AI, which will shape the future of healthcare.

1. AI in Drug Discovery: AI will continue to simplify drug discovery, shortening development times and accelerating the introduction of new therapeutics to the market.

Second, Predictive Analytics will advance thanks to artificial intelligence, allowing for more accurate forecasting of disease outbreaks and patient outcomes.

Self-management of chronic illnesses can be enhanced by the use of AI-powered virtual health assistants, which provide individualised healthcare guidance and assistance to patients.

4. Robotic Surgery: Using less intrusive and more precise methods, surgical robots powered by AI will revolutionise the field.

5. Genomic Medicine: AI will play a pivotal role in decoding the human genome, thereby revealing the genetic basis of disease and enabling the development of targeted therapeutics.

Wearable gadgets that use AI to track health in real time and deliver alarms and treatment in the moment are the future.

Blockchain technology will improve data security and patient consent management, allowing for data sharing while protecting privacy.

Overall, Big Data and AI are leading to a revolution in healthcare by allowing for more precise diagnoses, individualised treatment regimens, and enhanced health outcomes. The future of healthcare is inextricably linked to these game-changing technologies, despite the fact that there are serious concerns that must be addressed in the areas of data privacy, bias, and regulation. A more efficient, effective, and patient-centric healthcare system will continue to take shape as a result of the continued collaboration between healthcare professionals, researchers, and technology innovators.

Chapter 6:
Modern Media and Entertainment

6.1- Streaming platforms and the future of TV and film

What the Future Holds for TV and Movies on Streaming Services

The proliferation of online streaming services has had a profound effect on the television and film industries in recent years. Netflix, Amazon Prime Video, Disney+, Hulu, and others have given traditional cable and satellite TV services a run for their money. Because of this transformation, the entertainment industry has had to adapt its methods of creation, distribution, and management. We'l examine the pros, cons, and developing trends of streaming services and their effect on the future of television and film.

The Explosion of Online Streaming Services

The advent of streaming services has completely altered the media consumption landscape. Streaming platforms provide a wide collection of information that can be accessed at any time, from anywhere, and on any device, in contrast to traditional television where viewers were confined by schedules and limited choices. Several major changes have resulted from this shift:

Content Variety: Streaming services provide a wide selection of films, TV shows, documentaries, and even foreign productions. This selection is aimed at pleasing a wide range of consumers' individual preferences.

2. On-Demand Streaming: Viewers can choose when and where to watch material. They have the ability to control the pace of the video by pausing, rewinding, and skipping ahead.

Thirdly, viewers from all over the world have access to content because to the availability of streaming platforms in every country.

4. Original Content: Streaming providers are making significant financial investments in original programming, resulting in critically acclaimed and award-winning television shows and films.

5. No Ads: Many streaming services provide ad-free viewing, removing any potential distractions from the material itself.

6. Recommendation Algorithms: Powerful algorithms that analyse user behaviour in order to recommend material to users based on their preferences.

The Benefits of Streaming Services for Television and Movies

Customers are happier because they have more say in what they watch, when they watch it, and how they watch it (see also: Consumer Choice).

2. Global Reach: Content makers can reach a global audience without negotiating foreign broadcasting partnerships, providing fresh avenues for promotion and monetization.

3. Diversity and Inclusion in Storytelling: Streaming services have increased visibility for marginalised people in the entertainment business.

Fourth, Production Quality: Due to rivalry amongst streaming providers, production values for TV shows and films have increased to near-cinematic levels.

5. Monetization: Streaming services can generate income through a variety of means, such as membership fees, advertising, and product tie-ins.

Data-Driven Insights, No. 6: Streaming systems gather useful data on user behaviour, assisting content creators in making educated decisions about what to produce and how to sell it.

Issues and Things to Think About

Despite the many positive effects that streaming services have had on the entertainment sector, they are not without their drawbacks.

(1) Content Overload: The sheer number of content can be overwhelming, making it hard for users to discover and choose what to watch.

Second, the price of several streaming service subscriptions may discourage some customers from maintaining them.

The proliferation of streaming platforms has fragmented the industry making it tougher for content creators to negotiate profitable arrangements and for users to access all of their favourite content in one location.

4. Digital Rights: The negotiation and management of rights for multiple locations and platforms can be complicated, as can the ownership of digital rights.

The open access strategy has allowed for lower-quality content to get awareness, yet streaming platforms have increased production quality standards, thus quality control is important.

Data privacy is an issue because of the potential for regulatory scrutiny and compliance hurdles that arise from collecting and using viewer data.

Future of Streaming and Emerging Trends

Several major developments will shape the future of video-on-demand services:

To set themselves apart from rivals, streaming services will continue to put significant resources into producing unique content.

Interactive Content 2: Interactive storytelling, in which viewers make decisions that have consequences for the plot, is growing in popularity.

Third, Live Streaming: Streaming platforms will rise in popularity, making it difficult for traditional broadcasters to keep up with the demand for live sports and events.

Cross-cultural storytelling and a wider variety of content can benefit from international collaborations and co-productions.

material Discovery, No. 5: Viewers will have an easier time navigating the extensive material libraries with the help of enhanced recommendation algorithms and content discovery features.

Adaptation of User-Generated Content: Streaming services, taking a page from YouTube's playbook, may include user-generated content as a method to engage users and stimulate creativity.

Virtual and Augmented Reality (VR and AR) technology may provide interactive storytelling and immersive watching experiences.

The Effect on Classical Media Like Television and Movies

The film industry has also been affected by the rapid expansion of streaming platforms, which has challenged established TV networks and cable companies. In this way:

The typical theatrical release window is being bypassed or shortened as film studios examine new distribution models, such as releasing films digitally first.

2. Creative Freedom: Streaming services provide producers more leeway to create stories in whatever way they see fit, leading to more original and varied content.

Thirdly, there is "competition for talent," as streaming services offer attractive contracts and new ways to express one's creativity, attracting away the best and brightest from more established studios and networks.

Fourth, Viewer Preferences: People increasingly prefer on-demand programming, so broadcast networks are responding by launching their own online video services.

Five, Film Festivals: Streaming platforms have become significant players in film festivals, buying up distribution rights for festival submissions and increasing the exposure of indie films.

Conclusion

The advent of streaming services heralded a new age in television and movies by giving audiences more freedom of choice, accessibility, and influence over their viewing habits. As a result, the entertainment sector will likely evolve in response to the new norms established by these platforms in terms of content production, dissemination, and consumption.

Despite issues like content saturation and market fragmentation, streaming platforms are constantly adapting to new trends and technologies in order to provide a better experience for their users. Innovation and competition in the streaming industry are shaping the future of television and movies in ways that will be good for everyone involved. The distinctions between old and new in the entertainment industry will continue to blur as more and more viewers turn to digital streaming.

6.2- The influence of social media on pop culture

How Online Communities Shape Popular Culture

The ever-changing face of popular culture has seen the rise of social media as a potent force that influences fashion, propels debate, and brings people together from all over the world. Social media has revolutionised our experience with everything from viral challenges to meme culture. In this investigation, we will look into the significant impact that social media has had on popular culture, analysing its effects on the arts, commerce, and public debate.

Entertainment Amplification

The rise of social media has made it possible for fans of films, TV series, and celebrities to interact with these brands in ways never before possible. Some of the ways in which popular culture is amplified through social media are as follows:

1. Real-Time Engagement: Fans may interact with entertainment content in the present by live-tweeting during TV broadcasts, uploading reactions to movie premieres, and sharing memes about pop cultural moments.

2. Fan Communities: Social media encourages the growth of active fan communities that use the medium to analyse, critique, and celebrate their favourite media. The prosperity and durability of a property may depend on the attitudes and actions of these groups.

3. Viral Challenges and Trends: The rapid spread of viral challenges and trends in pop culture, from dancing challenges inspired by songs to hashtag campaigns supporting social concerns, is facilitated by social media platforms.

4. Behind-the-Scenes Insights: Celebrities and production firms use social media to provide fans exclusive access to the making-of footage and other materials, giving them an insider's look and helping them feel more connected to their favourite artists.

Content Promotion: Artists, studios, and producers utilise social media to build anticipation for new works and interact with their audiences.

5. Niche Content: Content that may not have done well in more mainstream outlets might find an audience and a devoted following on social media.

The Changing Role of Social Media in Fashion

Platforms like Instagram and TikTok have become digital runways for trends and style inspirations, and this has had a major impact on the fashion industry. This is how social networking has changed the way people dress in popular culture:

Influencers on social media and in the world of fashion have risen to prominence as trend-setters, brand advocates, and disruptors of the established order of things in the fashion business.

2. Instant Trend Dissemination: Fashion trends and styles are distributed globally within seconds on social media, democratising the industry and making fashion accessible to a wider audience.

Thirdly, Brand Collaborations: Brands team up with celebrities and social media influencers to spread the word about their wares and attract more customers.

TikTok users in particular have helped popularise fashion challenges, in which they present their own takes on the latest trends in the fashion industry.

5. Sustainability Awareness: Social media has increased public knowledge of eco-friendly and transparent fashion practises, leading to increased action from major businesses.

The Rise of the Social Media Music Scene

Social media has had a profound impact on the music industry by opening up new channels of communication between musicians and their fans.

1. Discoveries Driven by Platforms: Sites like YouTube, SoundCloud, and TikTok have catapulted musicians to fame by giving them a platform from which to spread their work and attract an audience.

2. Fan Engagement: Musicians utilise social media to engage with fans by talking to them, giving them updates, and showing them behind-the-scenes looks at their work. Because of this personal connection, fans are more invested and loyal.

Thirdly, Livestream Concerts: Social media has become a platform for livestreamed concerts and performances, giving fans a front-row seat to their favourite artists' events from the comfort of their own homes.

Artists can reach a wider audience and delve into uncharted creative territory by teaming up with other musicians, influencers, and content providers on social media platforms.

TikTok has been the driving force behind viral music challenges, which have resulted in breakthrough success for up-and-coming musicians.

Discourse in Society and Its Effect on Key Opinion Leaders

It's no secret that social media has had a major impact on public discourse, changing the way we talk about and interact with a wide range of cultural and socioeconomic issues:

First, Activism and Awareness: Social Media amplifies social justice movements, promotes debates about societal concerns, and helps activists to mobilise support and increase awareness.

Political influence is the result of celebrities and influential people using their platforms to discuss politics, support particular politicians, and rally the public to take action.

Thirdly, Viral Phenomena: Niche subjects and issues can go viral on social media, resulting in widespread attention and calls for action.

Social media has given rise to a phenomenon known as "cancel culture," in which people and organisations are targeted for criticism after they make words or take acts that offend the public.

Educational Resources: Educational material: Educational Resources: Social Media: Social Media acts as a platform for educational material, providing resources on a wide range of topics and fostering self-education.

Issues and Moral Concerns

Although the impact of social media on popular culture cannot be denied, it does not come without risks and ethical concerns.

The quick dissemination of incorrect information on social media can cause confusion, panic, and even physical injury to members of the public.

2. Impact on Mental Health: Young people's mental health can be significantly impacted by excessive use of social media, comparison culture, and cyberbullying.

Thirdly, there is cause for privacy and moral quandaries about the gathering and use of user data by social media sites.

Concerns regarding the digital gap and its effect on cultural participation have arisen because not everyone has access to social media.

5. Algorithmic Bias: Social media algorithms can perpetuate prejudices and filter bubbles, preventing users from being exposed to alternative points of view.

What's Next for Pop Culture and Social Media?

Several major shifts and changes will determine how much of an impact social media will have on popular culture in the future:

First, the growth of smaller, specialised communities on social media platforms that serve a particular interest group or subculture. Second, Short-Form material: Short-form video material, such as that found on platforms like TikTok, will play a larger role in influencing future developments in the entertainment and trending industries.

Thirdly, Virtual Experiences, powered by VR/AR tech, will improve how we interact with virtual pop culture, such as virtual concerts, events, and immersive storytelling.

4. Diversity of Voices and Perspectives: Social media will keep amplifying a wide range of opinions and points of view, fostering diversity and representation in the entertainment industry.

5. Integration of Electronic Commerce: Social Commerce,

 where consumers may make purchases directly on social media, thus blending the content and commercial realms.

The restriction of content is a possible threat to the free flow of ideas and information, including discussions about popular culture.

In conclusion, the impact of social media on mainstream culture has been substantial and varied. It has broadened participation in cultural activities, changed the fashion and music sectors, and increased the volume of public debate. Despite its many positive effects, social media can pose risks to users' safety, privacy, and mental well-being. The way we experience, produce, and interact with the cultural phenomena that characterise our times will be shaped by the dynamic interplay between social media and pop culture as technology advances.

6.3- Video games and virtual reality as entertainment mediums

Entertainment Options: Video Games and VR

Video games and virtual reality (VR) have caused a revolution in the entertainment industry. Millions of people have been captivated by the possibilities presented by these interactive and immersive mediums, which go far beyond the confines of conventional forms of entertainment. Video games and virtual reality (VR) have come a long way from Pong to become potent narrative platforms, social hubs, and pedagogical instruments in their own right. The purpose of this research is to investigate the entertainment industries of video games and virtual reality by looking at their history, current state, and potential future.

The Changing Face of Video Games

Games have advanced greatly from their early days, when they featured pixelated graphics and limited features. Several watershed moments have highlighted video games' development as an entertainment medium:

1. Arcade Era: Games like Pong, Pac-Man, and Space Invaders first appeared in arcades in the 1970s and 1980s. The video game business has its roots in these coin-operated machines.

Second, Console Gaming: With the introduction of home gaming consoles like the Atari 2600 and Nintendo Entertainment System (NES), video games were more widely available.

The introduction of 3D graphics in the 1990s with titles like Super Mario 64 and Doom changed the gaming industry by making games more immersive and realistic.

Online Multiplayer: With the development of the internet, users are now able to interact with people from all over the world. Popular culture has been influenced by games like World of Warcraft and Counter-Strike.

The proliferation of smartphones has ushered in a new era of mobile gaming, making games like Angry Birds and Candy Crush Saga immensely popular.

Independent game studios rose to popularity during this time period, producing critically acclaimed titles like Braid, Limbo, and Hollow Knight.

7. Esports: esports, or competitive gaming, has grown into a multimillion-dollar industry with its own set of specialised players, tournaments, and devoted fan bases.

The Influence of Video Games

Video games have significantly altered the media landscape:

Video games have come a long way as a storytelling medium, and now they can provide stories and characters that are just as deep and nuanced as those found in books and movies.

2. Interactive Worlds: Games like Grand Theft Auto and The Legend of Zelda provide players with enormous, open worlds to explore, erasing the distinction between themselves and the game's protagonist.

Third, Cross-Media Integration: Popular video game franchises frequently spawn related media adaptations in other types of entertainment, such as films, books, and TV shows, illustrating their pervasive cultural impact.

4. Streaming and Content Creation: Sites like Twitch and YouTube have spawned a new generation of gaming influencers who provide commentary and insight to viewers as they play.

5. Teaching Resources: The usage of video games in the classroom has been called "gamification," and it has been shown to improve students' ability to think critically and solve problems.

6. Virtual Reality (VR) integration: VR has given gaming a whole new level of immersion by allowing players to be transported to fantasy realms.

The Emergence of Virtual Reality.

The use of virtual reality in entertainment has progressed from the realm of science fiction to the mainstream. Virtual reality (VR) transports users to a digital realm, where they can participate in a variety of activities (from gaming to learning to interacting with others). There have been numerous eras in VR's development:

The first attempts at virtual reality (VR) were made in the 1960s, but the technology was too cumbersome and expensive to be widely used. Virtual reality did not become widely available until the 2010s.

The advent of the Oculus Rift and HTC Vive in 2016 was a major step forward in virtual reality technology, allowing for truly immersive experiences.

Third, Consumer VR: With the introduction of headsets aimed at the general public, such as the Oculus Quest and PlayStation VR, virtual reality has become more widely available.

4. Gaming and Beyond: Virtual reality (VR) isn't just for games; it's also utilised for things like travel, education, and even treatment.

Fifth, Social VR: Platforms like VRChat and Facebook Horizon offer social areas where users can connect in VR, expanding the scope of possible social interactions.

Virtual reality's influence on the entertainment industry

In many aspects, virtual reality is set to revolutionise the entertainment industry:

First and foremost, Immersive Gaming; players can feel more present and in control of their virtual worlds by physically interacting with them in VR games.

Cinematic Experiences (2): Virtual reality (VR) has the potential to revolutionise the way we watch films and television by putting viewers inside the action.

Thirdly, Teaching and Learning: VR may be used to create lifelike simulations for training purposes in sectors as diverse as medical, aviation, and the military.

4. journey and Exploration: Users can experience journey to far-off lands and bygone eras via virtual tourism, all without leaving their homes.

Five, Therapeutic Uses: Virtual reality is being used for exposure therapy, pain management, and rehabilitation, all of which provide new perspectives on healthcare.

Issues and Things to Think About

Problems and factors exist in both video games and virtual reality:

One, Access: Some consumers may be excluded due to high entrance costs or a lack of necessary hardware.

restricting people's ability to try virtual reality and high-end games.

Second, the quality of the material is essential to the continued success of both platforms.

Motion Sickness: For VR to gain widespread acceptance, this issue must be resolved for some users.

Fourthly, there are Privacy and Data security concerns due to the fact that virtual reality platforms collect user data.

5. Health and Safety: Extended use of VR can have physical and psychological impacts, thus safe and healthy practises for using the technology are important to establish.

Entertainment in the Next Decade
In terms of entertainment, video games and virtual reality have a bright future:

One, Advanced VR: As the technology develops, VR experiences will become more lifelike and immersive.

Cross-Platform Play (2): As virtual reality (VR) and more traditional gaming systems become more interoperable, players will be able to enjoy multiplayer experiences regardless of the platform they are using.

Third, Interactive Storytelling: Virtual reality (VR) and gaming will keep erasing boundaries between the two.

Fourth, Accessibility: Attempts to lower the price and increase the ease of use of VR will increase its popularity.

5. Innovation: Designers will test the limits of both video games and VR by introducing novel gameplay mechanics, environments, and narratives.

Finally, it is important to note that the cultural, social, and economic effects of video games and virtual reality go far beyond the initial interest groups for which they were originally designed. They have revolutionised the ways in which we enjoy leisure time, education, and communication. These forms of media are shaping the future of entertainment because they provide audiences with engaging, interactive, and original content that pushes the boundaries of what we consider to be entertainment.

Chapter 7:
Urban Planning and Smart Cities

7.1- IoT and its role in creating smart cities

The Impact of IoT on the Development of Smart Cities

The concept of "smart cities" has gained traction as a way to handle the complex issues of urban living in our increasingly urbanised world. Technology in so-called "smart cities" is used to raise living standards, reduce environmental impact, and maximise efficiency. The Internet of Things (IoT) is at the centre of this shift, as it is a network of interconnected devices and sensors that collect and exchange data to improve urban performance, adaptability, and sustainability. In this investigation, we will look into how the Internet of Things (IoT) contributes to the development of smart cities by analysing its advantages, disadvantages, and potential moving forward.

Smart city internet of things comprehension

The term "Internet of Things," or "IoT" for short, is used to describe the global infrastructure of interconnected electronic gadgets, sensors, and other systems that are able to exchange information and coordinate their actions. Commonplace items like streetlights and traffic cameras sit alongside more advanced sensors that track everything from air quality to energy usage to vehicular traffic. Real-time data collection, processing, and analysis are the foundation of the Internet of Things and are what make it so effective at helping cities make decisions and take action.

IoT's Positive Effects on "Smart" Municipalities

Smart cities may make better use of resources like electricity, water, and transportation thanks to the Internet of Things. Sensors can track the amount of energy used by a building's heating, cooling, and lighting systems and make adjustments to save money.

Second, Better Traffic Management is possible with the help of IoT sensors and cameras by keeping an eye on traffic patterns and congestion in real time. Using this information, cities may better time traffic lights, redirect cars, and ease congestion.

IoT devices allow for the installation of surveillance cameras, gunshot detectors, and emergency response systems, all of which contribute to increased public safety in cities. Better incident response is possible with the use of these technologies for police.

4. Waste Management: Smart trash cans with Internet of Things (IoT) sensors can provide signals when they need to be emptied, cutting down on wasteful collections and improving truck routes.

Environmental Sustainability Air quality Pollution Weather IoT Enables all of these measurements! This information can help shape environmental protection policies and programmes.

Smart Street Lighting, which is managed by the Internet of Things, may dim or brighten based on the time of day and the volume of traffic, thereby lowering energy consumption and the negative effects of light pollution.
Providing real-time data on public transportation, air quality, and other city services via mobile apps and websites is one way that Internet of Things (IoT) applications may engage citizens.

Issues and Things to Think About

Although there are many benefits to using IoT in smart cities, there are also some obstacles to overcome.

Concerns about data privacy and security may arise due to the collection and transmission of data from IoT devices. Strong citywide cybersecurity measures are a must.

Interoperability is another issue with the Internet of Things since devices from various manufacturers may employ incompatible communication protocols.

Building the required Internet of Things infrastructure and installing sensors across a city can be expensive and may call for significant investment.

4. Scalability: The IoT network must expand as cities expand. Future growth must be planned for.
Fifth, the Digital Divide makes it difficult to guarantee that all inhabitants can take part in and benefit from smart city programmes.
Smart city Internet of Things use cases
1) Smart Transportation: Internet of Things (IoT) sensors installed in traffic lights, public transportation vehicles, and roads aid in traffic management, congestion reduction, and enhanced public transit. Commuters have access to real-time data that can be used to better plan their routes.

The second type of environmental monitoring involves the use of sensors and other devices to keep tabs on things like air quality, pollution levels, and the weather. This information improves the ability of cities to deal with weather emergencies and informs environmental policy.

Thirdly, Energy Management makes use of IoT to keep tabs on and regulate how much power is utilised by various structures and public light fixtures. Smart grids improve energy efficiency, cutting down on both waste and expenses.

4. Waste Management: Sense-enabled trash cans send out notifications to garbage pick-up crews when they're full. This eliminates the need for costly pickups and eliminates waste. Fifthly, Public Safety is improved by IoT-enabled surveillance cameras, gunshot detectors, and emergency response systems because they give law enforcement and first responders access to up-to-the-minute data.

IoT improves water management by allowing cities to track usage, locate leaks, and control water mains with more precision.
7. Urban Planning: IoT data helps in developing and planning cities. This data can help cities make smarter choices regarding land use, transportation, and other municipal services.

The Impact of the Internet of Things on the Development of Smart Cities of the Future

The Internet of Things has limitless promise for the future of smart cities:

1. 5G communication: The introduction of 5G networks will offer quicker and more dependable communication, allowing for the unobtrusive sharing of data between Internet of Things gadgets.

2. Artificial Intelligence and Machine Learning: Cities will be able to analyse massive datasets and generate predictions for better resource management with the help of AI and machine learning algorithms that are integrated into the systems.
Thirdly, Edge Computing moves processing closer to the point of data creation, which improves latency and allows for quicker decisions to be made in real time.

Autonomous Vehicles, developed with the help of the Internet of Things, might completely alter the way people get around in smart cities.

5. Healthcare and Wellness: IoT will improve healthcare services by enabling remote monitoring of patients, tracking disease outbreaks, and promoting wellness through wearable gadgets.

6. Smart Grids: State-of-the-art smart grid technologies will make it easier to incorporate renewable energy sources, making urban areas greener and less carbon intensive.

Citizen-Centric Solutions: In the future, IoT projects will aim to increase residents' happiness by bettering their access to and use of city services and by promoting a stronger feeling of community.

Conclusion

The Internet of Things is important to the evolution of cities into "smart" environments. Smart cities use data analytics and the processing power of connected devices to better manage municipal resources, provide better public services, and make their communities more eco-friendly, cost-effective, and pleasant places to live. The future of IoT in smart cities has immense promise for developing urban areas that are better suited to satisfy the demands of their residents and manage the complexity of the modern world, while obstacles such as data privacy and interoperability must be addressed. Inevitably, as technology develops more, the impact of IoT on the cities of the future will grow and change.

7.2- Sustainable urban development through digital innovation

The Role of Digital Innovation in Promoting Sustainable Urbanisation

As urbanisation spreads rapidly around the globe, cities everywhere are encountering previously unseen difficulties. In 2050, the UN projects that approximately 70% of the world's population will be residing in urban regions. This fast urbanisation puts a strain on resources and infrastructure, as well as increasing pollution and traffic congestion. Sustainable urban development is becoming a top priority to combat these issues, and technological innovation is emerging as a potent weapon for advancing this cause. We'll look into what it means for cities and how digital innovation is helping to shape them for a more sustainable future as part of our investigation into sustainable urban development.

Learning About Eco-Friendly City Planning

The goal of sustainable urban development is to ensure that future generations will be able to meet their own requirements without jeopardising the present generation's ability to do so. It aims to construct cities that are sustainable from an economic and environmental standpoint while also welcoming to all members of society. Among the most important guidelines for creating sustainable cities are:

Environmental Sustainability: minimising resource consumption, minimising pollution, and maximising conservation to lessen cities' impact on the natural environment.

2. Economic Viability: Promoting economic growth and prosperity through environmentally responsible corporate practises, the production of new jobs, and the development of new infrastructure.

Thirdly, Social Equity is the commitment to improving the lives of all city residents via planning and building that prioritises accessibility, affordability, and inclusion in all aspects of city life.

4. Resilience: enabling urban areas to endure and rebound from disturbances like earthquakes and economic slumps.

What Part Does Digital Innovation Play?

Cities' approaches to sustainable development are being completely transformed by digital innovation, fueled by technological and data analytics advancements. The following are only a few of the most important domains where digital innovation is having a profound effect:

One example of a technology made possible by digital advances is the development of "smart infrastructure" designed to keep tabs on, analyse, and improve urban life in all its forms. There are also transportation networks, water management systems, and smart grids in this category. Congestion is alleviated, traffic flows more smoothly, and less fuel is used thanks to clever traffic management technologies.

2. Renewable Energy: Cities can make better use of renewable energy sources thanks to the incorporation of digital technology into the production and distribution of energy. Energy supply and demand can be balanced via smart grids, leading to less pollution and a longer lifespan for the power grid.

Thirdly, Data Analytics can help with urban planning and resource allocation by compiling and analysing data from diverse sources like Internet of Things (IoT) sensors, social media, and mobile apps. A good example of data-driven decision making is the monitoring of air quality for the purpose of reducing pollution.

4. Urban Mobility: Ridesharing platforms, electric vehicles, and autonomous transportation systems are reshaping urban mobility thanks to digital innovation. In addition to improving public transportation's productivity, these innovations lessen road congestion and greenhouse gas emissions.

5. Waste Management: Sensors and tracking devices built into smart waste management solutions improve the efficiency of garbage pickup times and locations. This lessens the need for fuel, cuts down on operational costs, and diminishes the negative effects of trash removal on the environment.

6. Green Building Design: Architects and engineers may create sustainable, energy-efficient buildings with the aid of building information modelling (BIM) and digital design tools. These innovations lessen a building's environmental footprint and cut down on energy use over its entire service life.

7. Community Engagement: Digital platforms allow local governments and inhabitants to more easily communicate and participate in one another's lives. Plans for urban development can be made more in tune with community needs and values with the help of citizen feedback and involvement.

Stories of Urban Sustainability's Greatest Achievements

Through technological innovation, some cities throughout the world are paving the way for future sustainable urban growth. Some instances are as follows:

(1) Copenhagen, Denmark: Copenhagen has become one of the most bike-friendly cities in the world. Incorporating real-time data on bike lane usage, digital innovation helps city planners optimise bike routes and enhance safety.

Second, Amsterdam, Netherlands: Smart parking systems in Amsterdam give drivers up-to-the-minute data on open spots, cutting down on the time spent in vain circling for a spot and the pollution that results from it.

Third, Singapore; this city-state is widely recognised for its innovative approach to urban planning. The city-state is a frontrunner in sustainable urban development thanks to its use of data analytics to track and improve utilities like electricity and water use, garbage collection, and public transit.

The United Arab Emirates' Masdar City is an example of a smart, eco-friendly metropolis that aims to minimise its impact on the environment. It has intelligent power grids, driverless electric shuttles, and a streamlined garbage disposal system.

5. Medelln, Colombia: Medelln has leveraged digital innovation to provide public transit accessibility for low-income communities by installing cable car systems and escalators in steep neighbourhoods. This has allowed more people to get to school and work.

Issues and Things to Think About

There is much promise in digital innovation for green city building, but there are also important factors to consider.

First, the Digital Divide: It is essential to ensure that all citizens have access to digital services and benefits so that current disparities are not exacerbated.

2. Privacy and Security: Strong cybersecurity measures are needed to secure sensitive information and retain public trust when collecting and managing massive amounts of data.

Third, interoperability: making sure different digital systems and technologies can talk to one another and work together is crucial for improving urban procedures.

To determine how data is collected, shared, and used while protecting privacy and ethics, cities need to establish explicit data governance frameworks.

The development of standardised criteria for measuring sustainability and assessing the impact of digital technologies is crucial for monitoring development.

Digital Innovation and the Future of Sustainable Urban Development

Digital innovation holds great potential for a bright and active future in sustainable urban development:

1. Artificial Intelligence and Machine Learning: Better analysis of massive datasets and smarter allocation of city resources will be made possible by recent advances in AI and ML.

2. Decentralised Energy: Rooftop solar panels and microgrids are examples of decentralised energy production that will allow cities to create and distribute clean energy locally while decreasing their reliance on traditional, central power facilities.

Thirdly, the Circular Economy, where materials are reused, recycled, and repurposed to reduce waste and preserve finite supplies, will be facilitated by technological advancements.

(4) Resilience Planning: Cities will invest in digital tools and technology to increase resilience against climate change and other risks, protecting their citizens from harm.

5. Global Collaboration: Cities all over the world will work together and share the most effective strategies for implementing sustainable urban development, speeding up the process and learning from one another's mistakes along the way.

In conclusion, resilient, efficient, and ecologically responsible cities can be built through sustainable urban development enabled by digital innovation. The increasing urbanisation of human populations increases the urgency of finding new approaches to urban problems. Cities can lead the way towards a sustainable future, where urbanisation and environmental preservation may coexist peacefully, by making use of digital technologies. Our cities will be preserved for future generations thanks to the constant efforts and developments in this field, which are transforming them in positive ways.

7.3- Data-driven decision-making in urban planning

Urban Planning Based On Hard Data

More than half of the world's population now resides in urban areas, making urbanisation a defining worldwide trend of the 21st century. Keeping up with the ever-changing needs of a city's infrastructure is a complicated endeavour that calls for well-considered planning decisions. Data-driven decision making is a game-changing practise in urban planning that has arisen in the digital age. It takes advantage of the potential of data analytics, technology, and information systems to mould more effective, sustainable, and citizen-centric urban environments. In this investigation, we will delve into the merits, pitfalls, and potential future of data-driven decision-making in urban planning.

Acquiring Knowledge of Urban Planning Through Data Analysis

Data-driven decision-making in urban planning is the practise of developing plans, decisions, and improvements for cities based on data and analytics. To better understand the dynamics, trends, and difficulties of metropolitan areas, this method integrates data from a wide variety of sources, including sensors, satellites, social media, and administrative records. The foundations of urban planning decisions based on data are:

Data collection is the first step in every data science project, and it can be done using a variety of tools such Internet of Things (IoT) sensors, GIS, questionnaires, and mobile apps.

The second step, "data analysis," involves using data analytics and statistical methods to examine the information gathered.

Thirdly, we have Visualisation, which is the practise of making information easier to understand and share by displaying it in visual formats such as maps, charts, and dashboards.

Using decision support systems (DSS) and other modelling tools to simulate urban scenarios and evaluate the potential impact of alternative options is the fourth strategy.

5. Policy Formulation: Creating policies and plans to deal with urban issues and reach sustainable development targets using data-driven insights.

Data-driven decision making has several positive effects on urban planning.

1. Educated Choices: In order to make judgements based on evidence and insights, urban planners can benefit greatly from data-driven methods.

2. Efficiency: Data analytics may enhance the delivery of urban services while optimising resource allocation and reducing inefficiencies, resulting in cost savings.

Third, Sustainability: Opportunities for energy efficiency, waste reduction, and sustainable transportation solutions are identified through data-driven planning, which contributes to Sustainability.

In the face of natural disasters and climate change, cities can use data to analyse risks, plan for disaster preparedness, and increase resilience.

5. Improved Infrastructure: Data-driven insights may direct the design and development of urban infrastructure like transport networks and utilities, leading to improved functionality and lower maintenance costs.

Providing citizens with access to urban data and incorporating them into the planning process are two ways in which data-driven decision-making increases openness and public engagement.

Uses for Data-Based Determination Making in City Planning

1. Transportation Planning: Through real-time tracking and predictive modelling, data analytics can optimise traffic flow, minimise congestion, and improve public transportation systems.

2. Housing and Land Use: Data-driven methods aid in gauging housing demand, pinpointing prime development spots, and formulating cost-effective housing strategies.

Thirdly, Environmental Sustainability: Data is used by urban planners to keep an eye on the state of our air and water, to oversee the care of our parks, and to devise plans to cut down on waste and preserve our natural resources.

Data analytics can also be used to monitor disease outbreaks and improve the efficiency of healthcare services in the public sector.

Economic Growth: Cities can use data to identify major industries and investment opportunities in order to recruit enterprises, encourage entrepreneurship, and boost economic growth.

5. Crisis Management: Data-driven decision-making helps cities better deploy resources during crises, enabling for faster responses and more effective management.

Issues and Things to Think About

While data-driven decision-making has many advantages, it also has certain caveats.

First, we must prioritise the Data Quality by making sure all information is accurate and trustworthy. When data quality is low, decision making can suffer.

2. Data Privacy: It is difficult to strike a balance between the necessity for data collecting and privacy concerns. Cities must adhere to data privacy standards and safeguard personal information.

Thirdly, the Digital Divide can make it so that not all members of urban populations can take advantage of data-driven planning.

Fourth, interoperability: It can be difficult to integrate data from different systems and sources. For effective data sharing, standardisation is essential.

5. Cybersecurity: It is crucial to keep urban data safe from cyber assaults. Cities need to spend money on strong cybersecurity measures to protect personal data.

Ethical Considerations(6) All data usage and decision making processes must be fair and equitable to eliminate any potential for prejudice or bias.

Data-Driven Urban Planning: Success Stories

Singapore is widely recognised as a frontrunner in the field of data-driven city planning. The city-state relies on data analytics to improve public services and infrastructure including transport and air quality monitoring. To better serve urban dwellers, "Smart Nation" projects use data from numerous sources.

To achieve its objective of becoming a carbon-neutral city by 2025, Copenhagen, Denmark uses data-driven decision-making.

Information on energy use, transportation trends, and air quality is gathered to help guide the city's sustainability initiatives.

Thirdly, Los Angeles, USA uses data analytics to deal with traffic problems. The city uses this data to adjust signal times, divert vehicles around accidents, and shorten travel times for residents.

Fourthly, in Amsterdam, Netherlands, a data-driven strategy for waste management has been put into place. When garbage cans are equipped with sensors that indicate they are full, collection schedules and prices can be optimised.

Data-driven decision making is the future of urban planning.

There is great potential for the future of data-driven decision making in urban planning:

First, Artificial Intelligence (AI) and Machine Learning: AI-powered algorithms will allow for more complex data analysis, predictive modelling, and scenario simulations, which will help with difficult decision-making.

Second, IoT (Internet of Things) integration: The proliferation of IoT devices and sensors will give real-time data on numerous urban characteristics, from air quality to energy consumption, improving the efficacy of decisions in these areas.

Blockchain, which provides transparent and tamper-proof data storage and sharing protocols, can boost data security and trust in urban systems.

4. Citizen-Centric Planning: Citizens will play a larger role in cities' data collection and decision-making processes, boosting openness and citizen input.

5. Global Collaboration: Cities all over the world will work together on data-driven urban planning initiatives, exchanging information, ideas, and best practises in order to address the problems that affect all cities.

In conclusion, data-driven decision-making is reshaping urban planning by equipping municipalities with the resources and knowledge to tackle intractable problems and propel sustainable growth. City planners now have more information and analytical tools at their disposal than ever before, allowing them to build safer, more efficient, and more pleasant urban environments. While there are still obstacles to overcome, there is no denying that data-driven urban planning has the potential to influence the future of our communities. It's an effective method that can help create successful, equitable, and environmentally friendly communities for all people.

Chapter 8:
Technology and the Future of Work

8.1- Remote work and the gig economy

The Impact of Telecommuting and the Gig Economy on Employment Trends

The advent of telecommuting and the growth of the "gig economy" have had a major impact on the nature of work in recent years. These two trends, which are frequently linked, have shifted the nature of work and given people more control over their careers and their lives. In this investigation, we will delve into the inner workings of telecommuting and the gig economy, analysing their effects on the modern workplace as well as its advantages and disadvantages.

Remote Work: A Better Understanding

Telecommuting, often known as teleworking, is the practise of doing job duties outside of a central office, most commonly from the comfort of one's own home. While some sort of remote work has been around for decades, the rise of high-speed internet and collaborative technologies has hastened its spread.

Important features of working from home are:

Benefit No. 1: Employees can have a healthier work-life balance thanks to the freedom to pick and choose when and where they put in their time.

Second, technological advancements have made it possible for distributed teams to function effectively. Tools like video conferencing, project management programmes, and cloud storage have proliferated in recent years.

Thirdly, Global Talent: Because of the flexibility of remote work, companies can find and hire the best people from all over the world, regardless of where they happen to be located.

Reduced travel costs, office overhead, and regional compensation differences are just a few examples of the ways in which remote workers and their employers might save money.

5. Productivity: Research has shown that workers who are able to set their own schedules and conditions at work may be more efficient overall.

A New Way of Working in the "Gig" Economy

The shift from permanent, full-time employment to temporary, project-based work is exemplified by the "gig economy," also known as the "freelance economy" or the "platform economy." Workers in the "gig economy" are self-employed or freelancers who do projects for various clients on a short-term basis (the "gigs").

Some essential features of the gig economy are:

Gig workers have more freedom because they can set their own schedules and work conditions. The ability to set one's own hours is appealing to anyone looking for a better work-life balance or a means to supplement one's income.

Second, "Digital Platforms": Gig workers frequently communicate with clients and customers through digital platforms and apps. The scope of these sites can be rather broad, encompassing everything from ridesharing to freelancing.

Thirdly, Diverse Roles: The gig economy includes many different professions, from drivers to designers to writers to consultants, and beyond. It opens up new possibilities for people to make use of their knowledge and abilities.

4. Income Diversity: Gig employment can serve as either a major or secondary source of income, allowing people to pursue numerous streams of income at once.

Managing their own enterprises and marketing themselves as independent professionals, many gig workers fancy themselves entrepreneurs.

Benefits and Drawbacks of the Gig Economy and Remote Work

Benefits for both workers and businesses can be found in the widespread adoption of remote work and the gig economy.

First, it promotes a healthier work-life balance by allowing people to spend less time at the office and more time with their families and friends.

2. More Job Possibilities: People can find ways to make money, advance their careers, and break into new fields by participating in the gig economy.

Thirdly, the Global Talent Pool allows businesses to discover the best people with the proper set of talents and experience for a certain project from all around the world.

4. Cost Savings: Remote work and gig work can result in cost savings for both businesses and employees, such as lower costs associated with renting office space and paying for transportation to and from work.

5. Flexibility: People have more leeway in determining their own work schedules and environments, which often results in more happiness and productivity on the job.

6. Entrepreneurship: People can follow their hobbies and make a living doing what they love thanks to the flexibility and freedom provided by the gig economy.

7. Innovation: The flexibility of remote work and the gig economy fosters creativity in organisational structures, tools, and practises.

Issues and Things to Think About

Although there are many advantages to working remotely and participating in the gig economy, there are also certain things to keep in mind:

The lack of face-to-face contact with coworkers can lead to feelings of isolation and loneliness for remote employees.

Concerns about security and privacy are heightened when remote workers access or store private information or personal documents outside of a traditional office setting.

Thirdly, it's important to set clear boundaries between work and personal life for remote workers to avoid burnout.

Because of the unpredictability of project-based work and the lack of benefits like health insurance and retirement plans, gig workers may experience income instability.

5. Benefits Access: Gig workers frequently lack access to benefits such as healthcare, paid time off, and retirement plans that are common in regular employment.

Concerns have been raised about the applicability of labour laws, the proper classification of workers, and the availability of necessary protections for gig workers.

Work in the Future: A Changing Landscape

Remote work and the gig economy are changing the nature of work itself.

1. Hybrid Work Models: Many companies are embracing hybrid work models that combine remote and in-person work to meet the needs of their employees and keep cooperation strong.

To facilitate remote work, it is essential to continue investing in infrastructure like high-speed internet and digital tools that can be used from a distance.

Work is more about outcomes than physical presence, thus employers are increasingly offering flexible work arrangements to attract and retain talent.

Fourth, employees in the gig economy and from home will keep spending money on training and education to improve their employability.

Governments and policymakers will struggle with the necessity to update labour laws and regulations to safeguard the rights and advantages of gig workers, which brings us to our fifth and last point: Policy and Regulation.

6. Entrepreneurship: The gig economy will encourage entrepreneurship, as more and more people see freelance work as a stepping stone to starting their own business.

Conclusion

Traditional employment paradigms are being challenged by the rise of remote work and the gig economy, which provide workers with greater freedom and independence. The COVID-19 pandemic hastened these developments by compelling businesses to embrace remote workers and speeding up the expansion of the gig economy. Both have their advantages, but they also present difficulties in terms of social interaction, physical safety, and financial stability. Workplaces of the future will likely combine online and in-person interactions as a result of technological advancements and shifting worker expectations. Individuals, businesses, and government agencies will need to be flexible and open to the possibilities offered by these revolutionary shifts in the workplace if they are to succeed.

8.2- Automation and AI in the workplace

Industry and Employment in the Age of Automation and AI

A new era of productivity, efficiency, and innovation has arrived in the workplace thanks to the advent of automation and artificial intelligence (AI). Industries are being disrupted, the nature of employment is shifting, and business processes are being revolutionised as a result of these innovations. In this investigation, we will look into the effects of automation and AI on the job market, discussing the pros, cons, and ever-changing nature of work in the twenty-first century.

Workplace AI and Automation: What You Need to Know

Automation is the process of using machines to do work traditionally done by humans. Data input is an example of a simple, repetitive operation that can be automated, while autonomous driving is an example of a sophisticated, decision-making process that may be automated. Robotic process automation (RPA), industrial robots, and software bots are all examples of automation technology.

AI, on the other hand, refers to the study and creation of computer systems that can carry out activities traditionally associated with human intelligence, such as perception of visual or auditory stimuli, decision making, and the translation of languages. Machine learning is a type of artificial intelligence that helps computers get better at their jobs over time.

Examples of the significant impact of AI and robotics on the workplace include:

First, automation and AI can enhance productivity and decrease mistake rates by performing activities more quickly and correctly than people.

2. Cost Savings: Businesses can save money by eliminating or lowering the demand for human labour by automating labor-intensive processes.

Thirdly, automated systems are scalable, meaning that they can take on more work without requiring a corresponding increase in staff.

Fourthly, Innovation: AI may propel innovation through the analysis of large datasets, the discovery of patterns, and the provision of insights for strategic decision making.

5. Improved Decisions: AI has the ability to sift through large amounts of data and give informed suggestions to decision-makers.

Sixth, better customer service thanks to AI-powered chatbots and virtual assistants available around the clock.

Advantages and Drawbacks of Robots and AI at Work

The widespread use of automation and artificial intelligence in the workplace has had far-reaching consequences.

Automation has had a profound effect on the manufacturing industry, resulting in greater accuracy, lower production costs, and higher product quality.

Second, the healthcare industry has benefited greatly from the use of artificial intelligence (AI) in the form of diagnostic tools and robotics-assisted surgery.

Financial data is analysed by AI algorithms for use in making investments, gauging risk, and uncovering fraud.

Four, Retail: Cashier-less stores and robotic warehouses are only two examples of how automation technologies have altered the retail landscape.

In the fifth place, we have Customer Service, where the use of chatbots and virtual assistants has drastically cut response times and increased speed and efficiency in helping customers.

6. Transport: Autonomous cars and drones are set to revolutionise transport and logistics by making them more secure and cost-effective.

Data Analysis: AI can analyse big datasets to discover insights, inform corporate strategy, and predict market trends.

Issues and Things to Think About

Automation and AI have many potential advantages, but they also raise certain concerns.

Job Displacement 1: Certain jobs, especially those involving routine, repetitive tasks, may be lost due to automation.

Two, the Skills Gap: workers may need to update their skill sets as the nature of their jobs changes. When workers lack the proper education and training, a skills gap can develop.

Ethical Concerns 3. AI introduces privacy, bias, and decision-making issues. It is crucial to ensure the ethical creation and application of AI.

4. Human-AI Collaboration: It can be difficult for businesses to strike the correct balance when combining human and AI efforts, as they must first establish clear boundaries between the two.

The rising usage of AI necessitates the collecting and processing of massive volumes of data, which raises questions regarding privacy and security.

Policymakers should adopt legislation to manage AI and automation while yet allowing them to contribute to innovation and economic development (see point #6).

The Changing Nature of Work

Work is changing as a result of the increased use of automation and artificial intelligence in the workplace.

While automation has the potential to eliminate some professions, it will also generate new opportunities in areas such as the design, operation, and management of automated systems.

Second, Human-AI Collaboration: Many tasks will require employees to collaborate with AI, and they will need to be able to work effectively with intelligent machines.

3. talents and Education: The future workforce will demand a more diverse collection of talents, such as technical proficiency, the capacity to solve complex problems, and the ability to quickly adapt to new situations. The need for continuous education is growing.

The spread of the COVID-19 pandemic hastened the trend towards remote work, and artificial intelligence (AI) plays a role in facilitating remote teams' ability to work together effectively and efficiently.

5. Customization: Automation and AI make it possible to better tailor products and services to individual tastes and requirements.

6. Global Workforce: By leveraging AI and automation, businesses can attract and hire top individuals from all around the world, eliminating many traditional barriers to entry.

The Importance of Learning

Education and training are crucial in preparing workers for the shifting job landscape as automation and AI transform the workforce.

First, it's important for workers to keep learning throughout their careers so they can maintain their competitive edge and flexibility in the workplace.

2. STEM Education: Science, technology, engineering, and mathematics (STEM) education will be crucial to equipping individuals with the technical abilities required in a society increasingly dominated by automation.

Skills in critical thinking, problem solving, creativity, and emotional intelligence will be in high demand in the future.

(4) Reskilling and Upskilling: Organisations and governments should invest in reskilling and upskilling programmes to assist workers in making career changes.

Workplace Robotics and Artificial Intelligence: The Future of Work

Key developments in the future of workplace automation and artificial intelligence include:

First, AI-powered decision help will become increasingly available to experts in a wide range of sectors.

Increased focus on AI ethics and regulation will help guarantee the responsible and ethical advancement and application of AI.

Third, AI in Healthcare: AI will continue to improve healthcare by enabling predictive analytics, personalised medicine, and robotic-assisted procedures.

Fourth, AI in Education: AI-powered educational technologies will offer students individualised lessons and aid teachers in their efforts to impart knowledge.

Fifth, AI in Sustainability: AI will help with sustainability by better managing resources and having less of an impact on the environment.

AI will play a vital role in cybersecurity by detecting and neutralising threats in real time (6th use case).

7. Artificial Intelligence and Augmented Reality (AR): The combination of these two technologies will improve several fields, including production, maintenance, and remote teamwork.

Conclusion

Workplace automation and artificial intelligence represent a sea change in the way we do business by opening up previously unimaginable avenues of effectiveness, creativity, and productivity. Despite these obstacles, the advantages of automation and AI can be seen in a wide range of sectors and businesses, altering the nature of work and necessitating a dedication to lifelong learning. Workers of the future will have the knowledge, abilities, and flexibility to operate side by side with automated systems in an atmosphere of mutual respect and cooperation. The influence of automation and AI will continue to shape the way we operate, solve issues, and propel progress in the twenty-first century as technology develops.

8.3- Upskilling and reskilling for the digital job market

Finding Success in Today's Digital Job Market Through Enhanced and New Skills

Skills and knowledge necessary for success in the modern work market have shifted significantly as a result of the digital revolution. Upskilling and reskilling are more important than ever as automation, AI, and other technological breakthroughs continue to transform industries. Here, we'll investigate the role that upskilling and reskilling play in today's digital job market, the opportunities and threats it poses, and the strategies that might help individuals and businesses thrive in it.

The Future of Work in the Digital Age

The digitization of industries has displaced long-established employment functions and necessitated the development of novel expertise. The digital labour market is characterised by many major tendencies:

One, the Emergence of New Roles: Data Scientists, Cybersecurity Analysts, Digital Marketing Specialists, and AI Engineers have all emerged as a result of digital transformation.

The Integration of Automation and AI: Data analysis to customer service, many industries now rely heavily on automation and artificial intelligence.

Thirdly, Cross-Functional Skills are in high demand since they allow workers to be successful in a variety of settings. For instance, the need for digital literacy among professionals in non-technical professions is on the rise.

Fourth, Remote Work; the COVID-19 epidemic hastened the widespread use of remote workers, making it essential that workers be able to collaborate digitally, communicate effectively, and manage projects effectively from a distance.

5. Continuous Learning: Due to the rapid pace at which technology is evolving, it is no longer possible to advance in one's profession without a commitment to lifelong learning.

Importance of Acquiring New Skills and Developing Old Ones

To stay competitive and relevant in the digital job market, upskilling and reskilling are crucial methods for both individuals and businesses.

First, we must address the skills gaps that exist across many industries, particularly in critical areas like cybersecurity, data analytics, and programming. These gaps can be closed by upskilling and reskilling programmes.

2. Career Mobility: People can use upskilling and reskilling to switch careers or rise in the ranks where they are already employed.

Third, by developing marketable abilities, employees can safeguard their careers against the elimination of their positions as a result of technological progress and automation.

Organisational Agility, or the ability to quickly and effectively respond to shifting market conditions, is enhanced when businesses invest in their workers' continued education and retraining.

5. Innovation: Employees who have received training to improve their abilities are in a better position to drive innovation within their companies.

Issues and Things to Think About

While it's easy to see why upskilling and reskilling are beneficial, there are still some obstacles to be aware of.

First, not everyone has easy access to high-caliber education opportunities, especially those living in underserved or rural locations.

The time and money required to acquire new skills can be a burden for people who are already juggling demanding professional and personal commitments.

Thirdly, Rapid Technological Change: Due to the rapidity with which technology is evolving, skills might become obsolete in a short amount of time, requiring constant retraining and adjustment.

To avoid further polarisation, it is crucial that everyone has equal access to chances for acquiring new skills and updating existing ones (see point #4, "Equity and Inclusion").

Fifth, Recognition of Prior Learning: It is essential to acknowledge and value knowledge and experience gained through non-traditional means, such as online learning and self-study.

Finding Your Way Through Retraining and Reeducation

Individuals and businesses should take the following preventative measures to succeed in the modern digital labour market:

To the General Public:

1. Self-Assessment: Evaluate your present-day abilities, strengths, and weaknesses. Think about what you want to get out of your career and how you can get there.

2. Determine In-Demand Competencies: Examine the digital labour market to pinpoint the in-demand abilities and knowledge. Research relevant job ads and market research.

Step three: make a plan for your upskilling or reskilling endeavours, detailing the exact abilities you wish to learn and the time frame in which you hope to accomplish them.

Choose Learning Pathways Look into a variety of educational options, such as traditional schools, online classes, bootcamps, and on-the-job training. Choose the alternatives that best serve your needs and situation.

Fifth, Never Stop Learning: Be open to the idea that education should be ongoing. Make it a habit to improve your knowledge and expertise by reading up on the latest developments in your field.

Sixth, it's important to establish and maintain professional relationships with other people in your sector. Insights and chances to hone one's abilities can be gained through networking.

For Institutions

First, Determine the Workforce Demand: Determine the full extent of your company's current and projected skill needs. Find out where you're lacking talents and make it a priority to learn new things.

2. Invest in Training: Dedicate funds to programmes that help you grow and develop your staff. Think about forming alliances with schools and virtual classrooms.

Third, instill a thirst for knowledge in your staff by encouraging lifelong education. Inspire your staff to look for ways to gain or switch careers.

Fourth, facilitate employees' development through the use of individualised plans that take into account both their professional goals and the demands of the company.

Fifth, establish mechanisms for monitoring and evaluating the results of training and retraining programmes. Measure and enhance their performance based on the results.

6. Supportive Environment: Foster a setting in which workers feel encouraged to continue their education. Give them your undivided attention, appropriate tools, and due credit.

The Importance of New Media and Distance Education

Technology plays a critical role in easing the process of skill acquisition and improvement.

1. Online Courses: Online learning platforms offer a wide selection of courses, typically at a fraction of the cost of traditional schooling. They let people to learn at their own pace and can be accessed easily, making them ideal for distance education.

Second, Virtual Labs provide a risk-free way to gain practical experience with technical abilities via simulations.
3. Artificial Intelligence Powered Recommendations: Some platforms utilise AI algorithms to recommend courses and learning pathways customised to an individual's goals and present skills.
Digital certifications and badges can offer concrete proof of skill gain and mastery.

5. Collaborative Learning: Learners can interact with teachers and classmates through virtual classrooms and collaborative technologies, building a sense of belonging and camaraderie.

Conclusion

There is constant upheaval and technological disruption in the digital job market. Upgrading and retraining are crucial tactics for success in today's dynamic business environment. Maintaining competitiveness and relevance in the digital era will necessitate a commitment to lifelong learning and the acquisition of new skills. Individuals can improve in their careers and businesses can develop a workforce ready to take on the challenges and opportunities of the digital future with the correct approach and investment. Proactively adapting to new circumstances through upskilling and reskilling is the key to a successful and satisfying job in the twenty-first century.

Chapter 9:
Cyber Risks and Online Dangers

9.1- The growing importance of cybersecurity

Cybersecurity's Increasing Importance

It is impossible to exaggerate the significance of cyber security in today's increasingly digital society. We are more susceptible to cyber assaults than ever before because of how deeply embedded our digital lives have become in the fabric of modern society. The expansion of internet-connected gadgets and the ease with which they may be used by cybercriminals have made it imperative for individuals, businesses, and governments to make cybersecurity a top priority. Here, we'll investigate the expanding significance of cybersecurity by looking at the changing nature of online threats, the results of cyberattacks, and the steps being done to protect our digital lives.

The benefits and drawbacks of the digital revolution are two-sided.

Life, work, and communication have all been altered by the advent of digital technology. It has revolutionised many facets of human existence, from productivity and communication to the availability of extensive knowledge at one's fingertips. The downside is that we are now more vulnerable than ever to cyberattacks because of our increasing reliance on digital systems.

The Changing Nature of Threats

As time has progressed, cyber threats have become more pervasive and complex. The ever-changing nature of the threats themselves, including:

Cybercriminals may now buy malware, ransomware, and hacking services on the dark web, a trend known as Cybercrime-as-a-Service that makes it easier for novice hackers to get started.

2. Nation-State Actors: With governments utilising cyber espionage and sabotage as tools of geopolitics, state-sponsored cyberattacks have emerged as a major worry.

Ransomware attacks, which encrypt data and then demand money from victims, have increased in frequency and severity in recent months. Data is encrypted by attackers, who then hold it hostage until a ransom is paid.

4. Internet of Things Vulnerabilities: The widespread adoption of IoT devices has resulted in the emergence of new security risks due to the widespread absence of adequate protections in place.

Phishing and other forms of social engineering are a common way for cybercriminals to get victims to give personal information or visit malicious websites (see also number 5).

Sixth, Data Breaches: Publicised data breaches have resulted in the exposure of sensitive personal and financial data, making victims vulnerable to identity theft and fraud.

Cyberattack Consequences

Cyberattacks can have far-reaching and devastating effects on individuals, businesses, and even entire nations.

Ransom payments, business interruptions, and the expenditures involved with remediation and recovery are just a few examples of the ways in which a cyberattack can lead to significant financial losses.

2. Reputation Damage: Companies that are cyberattack victims often see a decline in customer and investor trust as a result.

Third, Data Theft, which can result in identity theft, fraud, and privacy violations, is a direct result of data breaches exposing sensitive information.

Operational Disruption(4): Ransomware attacks, distributed denial-of-service (DDoS) assaults, and other cyber events can disrupt essential operations, resulting in considerable downtime.

Risks to National Security 5. Cyberattacks on essential infrastructure including power grids and water supply systems pose serious threats to national security.

Cyber espionage and the theft of intellectual property can damage a country's ability to compete economically and spur new discoveries.

Cybersecurity Awareness: The Human Factor

Cybersecurity relies heavily on technology, but human intervention is still essential. Awareness and education about cybersecurity are cornerstones of any good cybersecurity plan:

First, it's important to be aware of phishing so that you can spot attempts to gain unauthorised access and avoid opening malicious emails.

Second, practising good Password hygiene can help keep accounts secure by promoting the use of strong, unique passwords and multi-factor authentication (MFA).

Third, Social Engineering: Defeat social engineering by teaching people to be wary of providing personal information and to double-check the legitimacy of requests.

The danger of malware infections can be mitigated by encouraging safe online behaviour, such as avoiding dubious websites and downloads.

Encourage people to report cybersecurity incidents as soon as possible so that organisations can respond quickly and efficiently. 5.

Cybersecurity Precautions for the New Digital Frontier

Various cybersecurity methods and practises have arisen to counter the ever-changing cyber threat scenario, including:

To begin, there are technologies like firewalls and intrusion detection systems (IDS) that can monitor network traffic and prevent hackers from gaining entry.

Antivirus software is used to scan a computer for harmful programmes and then delete them.

Data encryption provides privacy even if sensitive information is compromised and accessed by an unauthorised third party.

Update your software and operating systems on a regular basis to close any security holes that could be used by hackers.

5. Network Segmentation: Cyber dangers can be contained by separating networks and limiting access to important information.

Organisations can better respond to cyber events if they have developed and routinely tested incident response plans.

Educating workers about the risks they face online and encouraging them to take precautions is the goal of security awareness training programmes.

Advanced Threat Detection, which uses machine learning and artificial intelligence to spot threats and suspicious activity.

The Role of Government and International Partnership

Protecting their own infrastructure and raising public and private sector understanding of the importance of cybersecurity are both critical roles for governments. The transnational nature of many cyberthreats makes international cooperation crucial as well.

To safeguard vital infrastructure and personal information, governments around the world are passing cybersecurity rules.

Second, "Cybersecurity Agencies" have been set up in several nations to coordinate all of the nation's cybersecurity operations.

Third, information sharing: governments and businesses working together to exchange threat intelligence makes it easier to spot and stop cyberattacks.

Fourth, International Agreements: Governments around the world are cooperating to create legally binding guidelines for appropriate online conduct.

5. Cybersecurity Diplomacy: Discussions on standards of behaviour and conflict avoidance in the realm of cybersecurity are rising in importance on the agenda of international diplomacy.

Cybersecurity: What's Next?

As time goes on and technology develops, cyber dangers will become more complex, and so will cybersecurity. The field of cybersecurity is evolving in response to several major trends:

Artificial intelligence (AI) and machine learning will play a crucial role in detecting and reacting to cyber attacks in real time (see also: AI-Powered Security).

2. Zero Trust Security: The idea that nobody should be trusted out of the box will gain traction, with a focus on constant authentication and monitoring.

The third factor is quantum computing, which may introduce new difficulties for encryption and necessitate the creation of quantum-resistant cryptographic algorithms.

The proliferation of 5G networks and Internet of Things (IoT) devices means that protecting them must be a top focus.

As more businesses perceive the value in insuring themselves against cyber threats, the market for cybersecurity insurance is expected to expand.

Conclusion

Cybersecurity is becoming increasingly crucial in the modern digital world. Cybercriminal capacities increase in tandem with technological development. Cyberattacks can have far-reaching effects on people, businesses, and even entire nations. To protect our digital lives, we need everyone from individuals to governments to take preventative measures in the realm of cybersecurity. The complex and ever-changing world of cyber dangers requires education and awareness, with strong cybersecurity measures and international cooperation. Cybersecurity isn't only a technical issue; rather, it's everyone's job to be vigilant, organised, and dedicated to the cause of keeping our digital lives safe.

9.2- Types of cyber threats and attacks

Classifying Cyber Attacks and Threats: Navigating the Cyber Warfare

The threats of the modern era have moved online from the actual world as a result of increased connectivity. The prevalence and sophistication of cyber threats and attacks pose a serious problem for all levels of society. When it comes to protecting our digital assets and fending off cyber attacks, knowledge is power. We'll look into a wide variety of cyber threats and attacks, dissecting their origins, goals, and effects in this investigation.

(1) Malware

Malicious software, or "malware" for short, is any programme with the intention of disrupting, damaging, or otherwise gaining unauthorised access to a target system. Typical forms of malicious software include:

- Viruses: Malicious software that replicates itself by infecting other files and spreading when the infected files are run. In addition to crashing your system, they can destroy your data.

- Worms: Worms are a type of malware that may replicate on their own by taking advantage of security holes in a network or computer system. They can spread swiftly and use up a lot of bandwidth.

- Trojans: Trojans pose as safe programmes but secretly perform malicious actions on the user's computer. They can be exploited to steal data, open doors for hackers, or cause other forms of damage.

Data encrypted by ransomware is inaccessible to the user until a ransom is paid. In return for the decryption key, attackers seek a ransom.

Spyware is malicious software that is installed without the user's knowledge and sends data about the user's computer activity to an external server.

Adware is software that shows ads without the user's knowledge or consent and typically generates cash for the attacker via ad clicks or impressions.

2. Phishing

In the fraudulent practise of phishing, fraudsters pose as legitimate businesses in an attempt to get personal information (such as passwords or bank account numbers) from their targets. It's usual for hackers to launch phishing attacks via:

- Email Phishing: Attackers send fake emails pretending to come from trusted senders in an effort to trick the recipients into visiting harmful websites or downloading malware.

This type of phishing, known as "spear phishing," aims to trick users into divulging sensitive information by sending them communications that appear to have come from a trusted source.

Sending phishing messages over SMS or other text messaging services is known as "smishing," and these messages often contain links to malicious websites or phone numbers to contact.

Voice phishing, also known as vishing, involves making fake phone calls in an attempt to trick victims into giving up personal information.

DDoS Attacks, Third

DDoS assaults, short for "distributed denial of service," are launched when several users simultaneously attempt to access a website, service, or network. The target must be made unreachable to authorised users. DDoS assaults can be carried out for financial gain, political reasons, or as a distraction for other forms of cybercrime.

Internal Terrorism

The term "insider threat" refers to someone within an organisation who have the potential to undermine security by abusing their position or access. Employees, independent contractors, and business partners are all fair game here. Theft of sensitive information, sabotage, or even carelessness can all constitute insider threats.

5. Man-in-the-middle attacks

Without the awareness of either party, a MitM attack can listen in on and perhaps manipulate the conversation taking place between them. In order to eavesdrop on or otherwise modify data, attackers place themselves in between the victim and the intended recipient. Public Wi-Fi networks and email communications are just two potential vectors for these kinds of attacks.

Component 6: "Zero-Day" Attacks

Attacks targeting vulnerabilities in software, hardware, or operating systems for which patches have not yet been released are known as "zero-day exploits." Zero-day exploits are frequently used by cybercriminals and nation-state actors to gain unauthorised access to systems or spread malware ahead of security measures being implemented.

7. Attacks on the Supply Chain

The goal of a supply chain assault is to compromise a good or service's security at the point of production, distribution, or creation of the code that runs it. Attackers insert flaws or backdoors into the supply chain that can be exploited later on.

8. Fudging the Credentials

When hackers utilise stolen credentials to access many accounts at once, they are said to be "credential stuffing." The fact that many users repeat passwords across many sites makes this practicable.

9. IoT Security Flaws

New vectors for cyberattacks have emerged with the explosion of IoT gadgets. Attacks or unauthorised access to networks can be launched using insecure IoT devices. One instance is the Mirai botnet, which targets Internet of Things (IoT) devices like routers and security cameras.

Social manipulation, number ten.

To achieve their goals, social engineers use techniques that play on people's vulnerabilities to persuade victims to give sensitive information or do other actions that benefit the attacker. Impersonation, persuasiveness, or emotional manipulation are common tools of this kind of attack.

11 APTs (Advanced Persistent Threats)

Advanced persistent threats (APTs) are state-sponsored or financially supported cyber espionage operations that last for years. Advanced persistent threats (APTs) use complex methods to hide in target networks, steal confidential information, and avoid detection for long periods of time.

Reasons for Cyber Attacks and Threats

Identifying possible dangers and prioritising cybersecurity solutions requires an understanding of the reasons underlying cyber threats and assaults.

Many cyberattacks, including ransomware and financial fraud, are motivated by financial gain (1). Those who launch attacks do so because they hope to make a profit.

Espionage, No. 2: Cyber espionage is conducted by nation-state actors to gain intelligence and a strategic advantage.

3. Hacktivism: Hackers engage in cyberattacks in order to draw attention to political, social, or environmental issues. Their antics could cause havoc in the workplace or in the government.

Data Theft: Cybercriminals frequently steal private information such as names, addresses, and credit card numbers in order to commit identity theft or to resell the information on the dark web.
5. Disruption: For political or ideological purposes, some attackers try to disrupt essential infrastructure, public services, or institutions.
Cybersecurity Precautions and Recommended Methods
The following cybersecurity measures and best practises can be implemented by individuals and organisations to protect themselves against the wide variety of cyber threats and attacks:

1. Regular Updates: Always use the most recent versions of programmes and operating systems, as well as any available security patches.

Use strong passwords (passphrases with at least eight characters) and enable multi-factor authentication (MFA) whenever it's an option for a given service.

Thirdly, raise people's awareness of security issues by teaching them about phishing and social engineering.

Fourth, use firewalls and good antivirus software to protect your system from malicious programmes.

Fifth, Access Controls: Set up permissions and authentication to limit who can access sensitive data.

6. Incident Response Plan: Create and exercise a plan to respond to cyber incidents in a timely and efficient manner.

7. Data Encryption: Encrypt private information before sending or storing it to prevent prying eyes.

Eighth, Regular Backups: Back up important data and systems on a regular basis to lessen the blow of ransomware or data loss.

9. Network Segmentation: Divide networks into smaller parts to prevent attacks from spreading laterally.

Tenth, in the supply chain, it is important to evaluate and guarantee the safety of all third-party vendors and suppliers.

Conclusion

The complexity of cyber threats and attacks in the modern day is a constant problem. Cybercriminals' methods and goals will change in tandem with the development of new technologies. Recognising the many forms of cyberattacks

essential for people, businesses, and governments to keep their data safe online. Measures and best practises in cyber security, along with constant vigilance and education, are crucial for mounting an effective defence against the ever expanding cyber threat landscape. Safeguarding our digital future is not only a technical issue; it is everyone's duty and calls for concerted action.

9.3- Strategies for protecting digital assets

Strategies for Safeguarding Digital Assets: Preserving the Electronic Pulse of Modern Life

In today's globally interconnected society, people, companies, and governments rely more on their digital assets. Everything from private data and inventions to vital computer networks is considered an asset. As cyber threats and attacks increase in sophistication and volume, the need to safeguard these digital assets has never been greater. Proactive cybersecurity tactics, risk management, and the significance of a cybersecurity culture will all be examined as we delve into the best methods for protecting digital assets.

Recognising the Worth of Digital Assets

Valued information, data, and systems have digital representations known as digital assets. They include a wide variety of tools, such as:

One example of personal information is a person's Social Security number, credit card details, or medical history.

Business Information: Companies rely on data such as client lists, financial documents, and original works of creativity stored in digital form.

Thirdly, Critical Infrastructure consists of digital systems that manage electricity distribution, water purification, and transportation.

Fourth, Intellectual Property: Patents, trade secrets, and proprietary information are all valuable resources for creating new products and staying ahead of the competition.

5. Online Presence: It is essential to have a website, social media profiles, and other online marketing assets to increase brand awareness and encourage customer participation.

The Changing Nature of Danger

The ever-changing nature of threats highlights the critical nature of taking precautions to safeguard digital assets, such as:

1. Cyberattacks: Cybercriminals use a wide range of techniques, including malware, phishing, and distributed denial of service attacks, to steal information and damage systems.

Attacks using ransomware encrypt data and hold it hostage until a payment is made to unlock it.

Third, Insider Threats: Data theft, sabotage, and inadvertent activities by malicious or careless insiders represent a serious threat to digital assets.

Fourth, Supply Chain Attacks: Attackers infiltrate supply chains to compromise product and service security from the ground up.

Five, Nation-State Actors: Political actors, spies, and saboteurs all benefit from state-sponsored cyberattacks.

Protecting Digital Assets in an Efficient Manner

Organisations and people alike should implement the following measures to lessen the impact of these threats and better safeguard their digital assets:

Create a Cybersecurity Mindset

A culture of cybersecurity begins with education and permeates every facet of a company's or an individual's relationship with technology. Important parts consist of:

- Training and Education: Consistently instruct workers or users about the perils, best practises, and significance of cybersecurity training and education.

Implementing well-defined policies and processes for cybersecurity that outline appropriate conduct is essential.

Define who does what in regards to cybersecurity, and who is on which incident response teams.

Create a culture of cybersecurity awareness and fast reporting of suspicious activity by staff and users.

(2) Establish a System for Risk Management

Cybersecurity risk management is a methodical process of recognising threats, evaluating their severity, and developing plans to deal with them.

Assess the organization's digital assets, vulnerabilities, and threats on a regular basis as part of the risk assessment process.

- Prioritisation: Create a targeted risk mitigation strategy by ranking hazards according to their impact and likelihood.

To lessen the blow of cyberattacks, it's important to design an incident response plan and put it through frequent tests.

- Monitoring and Detection: Establish mechanisms for constant cyber threat monitoring and detection.

Thirdly, Authentication and Secure Access

Protecting data in the digital realm requires restricted access and reliable authentication methods:

- Access Controls: Set up authorization rules and user roles to limit who can access what.

Use Multi-Factor Authentication (MFA) on all critical accounts and infrastructure.

- Password Hygiene: Require users to use complicated and unique passwords and urge them to do the same.

4. Encryption of Data

Encryption is a crucial tool for keeping private information that way:

Data encryption during storage helps deter hackers from accessing sensitive information.

Data-in-transit encryption involves encrypting information while it travels over a network or between devices.

5. Routine updates and fixes

It is essential to always use the most recent versions of software, operating systems, and security updates.

- Vulnerability Management: Conduct routine scans to identify security flaws and implement fixes as soon as possible.

Avoid using End-of-Life software, as it may no longer receive updates to keep it secure.

The Sixth Segmentation of Networks

Protecting vital resources from attacks requires segmenting networks.

To reduce vulnerability to attacks, it is important to isolate sensitive data from the rest of the network.

- Micro-Segmentation: Use micro-segmentation to regulate and keep tabs on communications between individual resources.

Recovery from Emergencies and Past Disasters

Always have a solid disaster recovery strategy in place, and back up your digital assets on a regular basis:

To ensure recovery in the event of data loss, it is important to perform regular backups of vital data and systems.

Backups and disaster recovery plans should be tested on a regular basis to ensure they are working properly.

Security in the Supply Chain and with Vendors

Evaluate and guarantee the safety of supply chain partners, such as vendors and suppliers, by performing the following:

To discover vulnerabilities, it is important to conduct security audits of vendors and suppliers.

- Security Agreements: Create legally binding documents that outline standards for cyber protection.

9. Recovering From Disasters

Create a plan for handling cyber issues quickly:

An Incident Response Team should be established to handle emergency situations.

- Communication Plan: Create transparent channels of interaction between stakeholders in the event of an issue.

10 Always Changing and Bettering

Maintaining a secure network constantly needs adjusting to new risks and technologies:

- Threat Intelligence: Utilise available threat intelligence sources to keep abreast of evolving cyber threats and security holes.

Cybersecurity testing, drills, and simulations should be carried out on a regular basis in order to assess and enhance existing security measures.

Conclusion

A proactive strategy, risk management, and a cybersecurity culture are essential to the protection of digital assets. Individuals, organisations, and governments must maintain vigilance and flexibility in their cybersecurity efforts as the threat landscape continues to change. The methods presented here can be used as a solid basis for protecting digital assets and decreasing vulnerability to cyber attacks. In today's technological age, safeguarding digital assets is crucial to preserving the safety and viability of our interdependent society.

Chapter 10:
Sustainability in the Environment and Cutting-Edge Technology

10.1- Green technology and its impact on environmental conservation

How Green Technology Can Help Save the Planet

As environmental threats and climate change define our period, green technology's evolution and widespread use have become indispensable to the cause of environmental preservation and long-term sustainability. The term "green technology," which also refers to "clean technology" and "eco-friendly technology," is used to describe a wide range of developments with the goal of reducing the harmful effects of human activities on the environment. In this investigation, we will look into the idea of green technology, as well as its many iterations and uses, and its far-reaching effects on ecological preservation.

The Urgent Need to Protect Our Planet.

Deforestation, pollution, habitat loss, and the worrisome growth in greenhouse gas emissions have thrust environmental protection into the global spotlight. Ecosystems, biological variety, and natural resources are the focus of conservation initiatives that seek to secure the future prosperity of humanity.

The following are major reasons why protecting the environment is so urgent:

1. Climate Change: Unprecedented changes in weather patterns, rising sea levels, and extreme weather events are being caused by

the rapid increase in global temperatures resulting from greenhouse gas emissions from human activities.

2. Biodiversity Loss: The loss of biodiversity has been caused by human activities such as the destruction of habitats, the introduction of harmful pollutants, and the excessive use of natural resources.

The third major problem is resource depletion, which is caused by the excessive use of finite resources including water, trees, and metals.

Air and water pollution: pollution from manufacturing and farming causes major problems for human health and ecosystems.

5. Economic and Social Impacts: Degradation of the environment can have serious economic and social effects, including the uprooting of entire populations and the destruction of their means of subsistence.

Green technology is a means to protect the planet.

Green technology is a radical departure from conventional methods of technological progress. It is concerned with finding answers that not only benefit people but also lessen their influence on the planet. The goals of green technology are:

1. Decrease Pollution: Green technology aids in lowering pollution levels by making use of greener energy sources and manufacturing processes.

2. Conserve Resources: New technologies allow for less wasteful and more efficient use of water and energy, for example.

Reducing greenhouse gas emissions and encouraging sustainable practises, green technology plays a significant part in climate change mitigation.

4. Preserve Biodiversity: Ecosystems and biodiversity can be better protected thanks to conservation efforts bolstered by environmentally friendly technologies.

To ensure that human activities do not affect future generations' ability to meet their requirements, green technology places a premium on sustainability.

Different Types and Uses of Eco-Friendly Technology

A broad range of inventions from many fields contribute to green technology, each with its own set of uses and advantages.

1. Sources of Sustainable Energy

Green technology relies heavily on renewable energy sources. For example,

- Solar Power: Solar panels convert sunlight into usable electricity that can power buildings of all sizes and even entire neighbourhoods.

- Wind Power: Electricity generated by wind turbines is a renewable and environmentally friendly energy option.

Hydropower facilities use the kinetic energy of moving water to create electricity, and when properly planned and operated, they have little effects on the surrounding environment.

Geothermal energy is generated by using the Earth's internal heat to generate electricity and provide space heating.

Biomass energy is the process of creating energy and heat from organic resources including wood, agricultural waste, and biofuels.

Using renewable energy sources helps minimise emissions of climate-altering greenhouse gases and our dependency on these resources.

2. Efficient Use of Energy

The goal of energy-saving technology and practises is to reduce power usage in a number of contexts.

Smart grids optimise electricity delivery, lowering energy waste and increasing dependability.

Appliances with the Energy Star label and LED lights are two of the best ways to cut down on electricity use around the house or company.

Energy efficiency and cooling expenses can be decreased by the use of sustainable building design and materials.

Improvements in energy efficiency cut down on carbon dioxide emissions, save money on power, and spread eco-friendly ideas.

3. Ecologically Sound Transport

The transport industry is undergoing radical change due to green technology.

Electric vehicles (EVs) produce less pollution and greenhouse gas emissions than conventional vehicles since they run on electricity rather than fossil fuels.

- Hybrid Vehicles: To reduce emissions and increase fuel economy, hybrid cars use a combination of electric and internal combustion engines.

Innovative forms of public transit, such as battery-powered buses and high-speed trains, help cut down on pollution and traffic.

Investment in cycling and walking infrastructure is a good way to encourage sustainable travel options.

Initiatives to green the transport sector aim to cut down on pollution, boost air quality, and cut down on oil use.

4. Recycling and Garbage Disposal

Improvements in garbage collection and recycling have cut down on trash in landfills and saved a lot of materials.

Technology advancements in the recycling industry have led to greater productivity and less waste.

Facilities that process municipal solid waste into energy instead of dumping it in landfills are called "waste-to-energy" plants.

To lessen the amount of methane released by landfills, composting organic waste is a great option.

Waste minimization and recycling campaigns help save natural resources and lessen the load on the environment.

5. Agricultural Sustainability

Sustainable agriculture is at the heart of green technologies.

Improved crop yields can be achieved with less water and fewer chemicals when precision farming methods are used.

Grow crops with little impact on the surrounding environment by employing vertical farming techniques.

- Organic Farming: By minimising the use of synthetic fertilisers and pesticides, organic farming improves soil quality and increases biodiversity.

Ecosystems can be better protected, resources can be conserved, and the environmental effect of food production can be lessened with the help of sustainable agriculture.

(6) Water reuse and recycling

The significance of green technology in water conservation is crucial:

- Water Recycling: State-of-the-art water recycling systems clean wastewater for reutilization in manufacturing, agriculture, and other sectors.

Water-scarce areas can benefit from desalination technology, which extracts potable water from saltwater or brackish water.

- Efficient Irrigation: Water conservation in agriculture and landscaping is achieved via the employment of sophisticated irrigation systems.

Combating water scarcity and protecting aquatic ecosystems need concerted efforts to conserve water supplies.

Effects on Protecting the Environment

Green technology adoption has far-reaching effects on environmental protection:

1. Reduced Emissions: Green technology in the energy sector, the transportation sector, and the industrial sector all lower emissions of greenhouse gases, helping to slow global warming.

2. Resource Conservation: Sustainable farming practises, wise water management, and recycling tools all contribute to a more conscientious approach to using the world's finite supplies of raw materials.

Thirdly, Biodiversity Protection is helped along by green technology since it encourages and facilitates sustainable conservation practises and policies.

Cleaner air and water are two additional environmental and health benefits that can be attributed to the use of green technologies.

5. Climate Change Resilience: Green infrastructure, such as green roofs and flood-resistant designs, increases resilience to the effects of climate change.

The green technology industry creates economic prospects, such as new job openings and groundbreaking discoveries.

Directions for the Future and Current Challenges

However, there are obstacles to implementing green technology's potential for protecting the environment:

Some people and businesses are put off by the high start-up and maintenance expenses associated with green technology.

Second, "infrastructure": "green" technology retrofits to existing infrastructure are notoriously difficult and expensive.

Thirdly, Policy and Regulation: Green technology adoption might be slowed by inconsistent policies and regulations.

Innovations in Technology

To make environmentally friendly technologies more accessible and cost-effective, continued innovation is required.

These issues must be resolved, sustainable practises must be encouraged, and a worldwide commitment to environmental protection must be fostered if green technology is to have a bright future. The relevance of green technology as a potent weapon for conservation and sustainability cannot be emphasised as the globe faces the serious concerns of climate change and environmental deterioration. The world and all its people will benefit greatly from its widespread implementation and continuous development.

10.2- Digital solutions for reducing carbon emissions

The Role of Digital Technologies in Mitigating Climate Change

The need to cut down on carbon emissions is more urgent than ever in light of the worsening global climate disaster. Rising greenhouse gas levels in the atmosphere are a primary driver of global warming and its accompanying repercussions, which in turn are exacerbated by our prolonged reliance on fossil fuels, inefficient industrial processes, and unsustainable transportation systems. From smart grids and energy-efficient buildings to data-driven transportation and sustainable agriculture, digital solutions play a crucial role in reducing greenhouse gas emissions, and we'll take a closer look at all of them here.

The Problem of Carbon Emissions

Human activities like these contribute to the release of greenhouse gases like carbon dioxide (CO_2) and others into the atmosphere.

Carbon emissions are mostly caused by the combustion of fossil fuels like coal, oil, and natural gas for uses including power generating, home heating, and vehicle fuel.

Industrial processes, such as those used to make cement and chemicals, generate carbon emissions as a byproduct of their chemical reactions and the energy they consume.

Deforestation and other forms of land-use change also contribute to carbon emissions because they lessen the planet's ability to take in carbon dioxide.

Methane (CH_4) is a powerful greenhouse gas that is produced as a byproduct of agriculture, including cattle production and rice cultivation.

Increases in carbon emissions have far-reaching effects, including the occurrence of more frequent and severe weather events, the elevation of sea levels, the extinction of species, and the disruption of ecosystems and economies. Sustainable practises, the use of renewable energy sources, and cutting-edge technology solutions are all part of a worldwide effort to address these threats.

Greenhouse Gas Reduction Through Digital Means

The use of digital technologies has been game-changing in the fight against carbon emissions. Optimising energy use, increasing resource efficiency, and spreading sustainable practises are all aided by these digital solutions' use of data, connection, and sophisticated analytics. Some of the most important domains where digital solutions are having an outsized effect are as follows:

1. Energy Management and Smart Grids

The introduction of smart grids has caused a sea change in the production, transmission, and use of electrical power. Data-driven technologies make possible:

By dynamically adjusting energy use in response to changes in supply and demand, smart grids can lessen the burden on peaker plants while increasing efficiency.

- Grid Optimisation: Utilities may optimise the distribution of electricity with the use of advanced analytics and sensors, which decreases transmission losses and boosts dependability.

Smart grids efficiently manage the intermittent nature of renewable energy sources like solar and wind, allowing for easier integration.

Smart metres and home energy management systems provide people the power to track and adjust their energy consumption and costs, which in turn reduces demand and carbon emissions.

(2) "Energy-Efficient" Structures

Both energy use and greenhouse gas emissions are significantly impacted by the building industry. For more energy-efficient buildings, digital solutions include:

- Building Automation Systems (BAS): BAS regulate lighting, HVAC, and ventilation to reduce power consumption in response to building occupancy and external environmental factors.

- Energy Analytics: Analysing data in real-time sheds light on trends of energy consumption, empowering building operators to make educated decisions that cut down on unnecessary energy use.

- Intelligent Sensors: Occupancy and environmental sensors aid in real-time adjusting of lighting and HVAC to user needs.

Building Information Modelling (BIM) is a tool that helps professionals like architects and engineers create structures that are both functional and environmentally friendly.

Third, eco-friendly transportation

The transportation industry is a key source of greenhouse gas emissions, but it is undergoing significant change as a result of digital solutions.

Cleaner alternatives to internal combustion engines can be found in the form of Electric Vehicles (EVs) when coupled with digital charging infrastructure and smart grid connectivity.

- Ride-Sharing and Mobility-as-a-Service (MaaS): Effective digital platforms for ridesharing exist, resulting in fewer cars on the road.

Commercial fleets can save money on petrol and time on the road with the use of GPS and telematics systems, which are used for fleet management.

- Connected and Autonomous Vehicles: By optimising routes and driving behaviour, autonomous vehicles can help lower emissions.

Agriculture and the Provision of Food

Emissions of greenhouse gases are substantial in agriculture, but digital solutions can improve sustainability.

Precision agriculture is a kind of farming that uses data to increase harvests while decreasing the amount of water and chemicals required to do so.

Farmers can better control animal health and cut down on methane emissions with the use of IoT sensors and data analytics with the help of livestock monitoring.

Transparency in food supply chains made possible by digital technology cuts down on spoiling and the emissions it causes.

5. Processes in the Industrial Sector

Industrial operations are becoming more efficient and environmentally friendly thanks to digital technologies.

Data analytics and machine learning optimise energy-intensive manufacturing processes to minimise environmental impact.

In order to reduce downtime and energy waste, equipment failures can be predicted with the help of sensor data in a process called "predictive maintenance."

The transition to a circular economy, where materials are recycled and reused, is aided by digital solutions.

6. Integrating Renewable Energy Sources

In order to maximise their incorporation into the energy system, renewable energy sources like solar and wind will need digital solutions to accommodate their rapid expansion.

Energy forecasting is the practise of predicting the amount of energy that will be produced from renewable sources in the future so that grid operators can prepare for this output.

By optimising the charging and discharging of energy storage devices, digital control systems improve the reliability of the grid.

- Grid Management: In an environment where intermittent renewables are present, grid operators employ digital tools to strike a balance between supply and demand.

7. Monitoring and Reporting of Carbon Emissions

With the use of digital tools, businesses can keep tabs on their carbon output and report those numbers accurately. Carbon accounting programmes, emission monitoring applications, and sustainability reporting websites all fall under this category of answers.

The Value of Digital Methods

There are many upsides of using digital tools to cut carbon output:

Emissions Reduction 1. Digital technologies help optimise processes, decrease waste, and minimise energy use, all of which lead to fewer carbon emissions.

2. Cost Savings: Businesses and consumers may typically save a lot of money by adopting energy-efficient practises and optimising their operations.

The third way in which digital solutions contribute to sustainability is through their emphasis on Resource Efficiency.

4. Resilience: Enhanced energy management and grid optimisation increase resilience to interruptions and power outages brought on by climate change.

5. Innovation: Digital technologies propel innovation in the energy, transportation, agricultural, and industry sectors, resulting in more eco-friendly methods of production.

Sixthly, Job Creation: The creation and implementation of digital solutions generates employment possibilities in the clean energy and sustainability industries.

Implications and Challenges

ations

While digital solutions have the potential to greatly cut down on carbon emissions, there are certain important factors to keep in mind:

First, the Digital Divide makes it difficult for these methods to be widely implemented.

Cybersecurity is a growing concern as interconnected digital systems become easier targets for malicious actors.

Privacy: Data privacy considerations must be addressed when gathering and analysing huge amounts of personal or sensitive data.

Interoperability, or the ability of different digital systems and platforms to communicate and work together, is crucial for a smooth rollout.

Conclusion

The war against carbon emissions and climate change as a whole is undergoing a transformation fueled by digital solutions. Energy consumption can be optimised, waste can be reduced, and sustainable practises can be spread throughout sectors by leveraging data, connectivity, and advanced analytics. Incorporating digital solutions into our daily lives and commercial activities is crucial if we are to achieve significant reductions in carbon emissions and protect the health of our planet for future generations.

10.3- IoT in monitoring and managing environmental resources

The Internet of Things for Conservation and Sustainability in Resource Management and Monitoring

The Internet of Things (IoT) has become a formidable ally in the monitoring and management of environmental resources in an era defined by environmental issues and the urgency of climate change. From agriculture and forestry to water management and wildlife conservation, the IoT's real-time data collection, analysis, and remote control capabilities have broad use. The Internet of Things (IoT) plays a crucial role in environmental monitoring and management, radically altering conservation efforts and presenting new difficulties and opportunities, all of which we shall investigate in this article.

The Current Environmental Crisis

Air, water, soil, biodiversity, and forests are all examples of environmental resources. However, these assets are threatened by a number of human actions:

One major cause of habitat loss, decreased biodiversity, and increased carbon emissions is deforestation, which occurs when forests are cut down for agricultural, urban, or logging purposes.

2. Water Scarcity: The world's freshwater supplies are under severe stress from rising populations and industry.

The third cause of decreased agricultural output is soil deterioration, which is exacerbated by the use of non-sustainable farming methods, soil erosion, and urban sprawl.

The loss of habitat, pollution, and climate change are all contributing to a precipitous drop in biodiversity that puts many species in jeopardy.

5. Climate Change: Rising greenhouse gas emissions are being driven by the burning of fossil fuels and deforestation, which in turn is causing global warming and its negative repercussions.

Internet of Things' Importance in Managing Natural Resources

When it comes to managing natural resources, the Internet of Things is revolutionary. To better monitor and manage our planet's natural resources, it use sensors, networking, and data analytics.

(1) Sensing the Environment

Sensors built into IoT devices allow for the monitoring of a wide variety of environmental factors, such as:

Air quality is monitored by sensors that detect noxious gases and particles in the air, such as PM2.5, NO2, and CO.

Water sensors measure things like pH, temperature, turbidity, and the presence of contaminants to determine water quality.

Precision farming and soil conservation benefit from soil sensors that track moisture, nutrient, and temperature.

- Climate Data: Using IoT sensors, weather stations report current conditions such as temperature, humidity, wind speed, and precipitation in real time.

IoT-enabled tracking devices are useful for tracking wildlife in order to observe their habits and patterns of movement.

2. Distant Supervision and Management

With the use of IoT technology, a wide range of environmental assets and systems may be remotely monitored and controlled, including:

- Smart Agriculture: Internet of Things (IoT) sensors in agriculture allow farmers remotely monitor soil conditions, water usage, and crop health, leading to more efficient use of resources and less waste.

Improved water resource management is made possible by the Internet of Things' management of water distribution, leak detection, and remote irrigation control.

Conservation efforts in forests can be aided by installing remote sensors and cameras to check for illegal logging, fires, and wildlife populations.

- Waste Management: Internet of Things-enabled trash cans provide actual volume to optimise garbage pickup schedules and cut down on gas usage.

(3) Predictive Modelling and Data Analysis

In order to gain insights and support predictive modelling, the vast amounts of data generated by IoT devices are processed using cutting-edge analytics and machine learning algorithms.

With the use of Predictive Analytics, environmental disasters like droughts, floods, and disease outbreaks can be anticipated and prepared for in advance.

- Resource Optimisation: Data analytics improve irrigation efficiency and lessen the need for fertilisers and pesticides, optimising the use of these valuable agricultural resources.

- Conservation Planning: IoT data is being used by wildlife conservation organisations to better conserve endangered species and fight poaching.

4. The Protection of Animals

The Internet of Things has been a game-changer for wildlife protection:

Collars and tags equipped with global positioning satellites (GPS) broadcast data in real time on the whereabouts and actions of animals, which helps conservationists.

Smart sensors, drones, and cameras aid in the detection and deterrence of poachers in wildlife preserves and other protected areas.

- Habitat Restoration: Internet of Things (IoT) technology helps in habitat restoration by tracking the development of reforestation and habitat improvement programmes.

5. Agricultural Sustainability

Internet of Things technology encourages eco-friendly farming methods:

- Precision Farming: IoT sensors collect information on soil, weather, and crop health to facilitate targeted and efficient agricultural practises.

- Livestock Management: By tracking animals' whereabouts and vitals, smart collars and tags help keep herds healthier and more productive.

Drones with Internet of Things (IoT) sensors can monitor agricultural growth and spot problems like pests and diseases.

Issues and Things to Think About

The Internet of Things (IoT) brings both exciting opportunities and important problems for natural resource management.

One of the biggest issues with the Internet of Things (IoT) is keeping people's data safe from hackers and private.

Interoperability, or the capacity of different Internet of Things (IoT) devices and systems to talk to one another and share information, is crucial to their usefulness.

Third, Sustainability is essential, as creating and discarding IoT devices might have negative effects on the environment.

4. Cost: The initial investment required to implement IoT solutions might be prohibitive, especially in places with limited funding.

5. Regulation: It is a challenging undertaking to create and execute regulations and standards for Internet of Things devices to guarantee that they adhere to environmental and ethical norms.

Case Studies: The Real-World Effects of IoT on Resource Management for the Environment

1. Smart Agriculture in California: IoT-enabled precision farming techniques have decreased water use, decreased pesticide and fertiliser use, and enhanced crop yields in California's agricultural sector.

Singapore's water distribution system is efficiently managed thanks to IoT sensors and smart metres, which has resulted in a decrease in water waste and a more reliable water supply.

Thirdly, Forest Conservation in Brazil, wherein video traps and remote sensors from the Internet of Things (IoT) aid in keeping tabs on deforestation and following the movements of Amazonian animals.

Animals in Kenya are safer from poachers thanks to Internet of Things-enabled tracking devices attached to elephants and rhinos.

Conclusion

The emergence of the IoT as a viable technology has

force for change in the field of managing environmental resources. Conservation initiatives, sustainable agriculture, and water management are just a few of the areas that have benefited greatly from its ability to capture real-time data, permit remote monitoring and control, and support predictive modelling. While issues like data security and cost remain, it is clear that IoT has the ability to aid in the preservation and responsible administration of our limited natural resources. The Internet of Things (IoT) has the potential to play a crucial role in environmental resource management as we continue to face the critical concerns of climate change and resource shortages.

www.ingramcontent.com/pod-product-compliance
Lightning Source LLC
LaVergne TN
LVHW021237080526
838199LV00088B/4553